NEGOTIATING CONVIVIALITY:
The Use of Information and Communication Technologies by Migrant Members of the Bay Community Church in Cape Town

Paula Louise Hay

Langaa Research & Publishing CIG
Mankon, Bamenda

Publisher
Langaa RPCIG
Langaa Research & Publishing Common Initiative Group
P.O. Box 902 Mankon
Bamenda
North West Region
Cameroon
Langaagrp@gmail.com
www.langaa-rpcig.net

Distributed in and outside N. America by African Books Collective
orders@africanbookscollective.com
www.africanbookcollective.com

ISBN: 9956-792-72-1

DISCLAIMER
All views expressed in this publication are those of the author and do
not necessarily reflect the views of Langaa RPCIG.

Acknowledgements

Firstly, to my supervisor Professor Francis Nyamnjoh: thank you for your guidance during my fieldwork and insightful and encouraging feedback throughout the writing process. Sheldon Kidwell: thank you welcoming me to the Bay Community Church and for your kindness and assistance throughout my fieldwork; Rowena Hay: thank you for your unwavering generosity, care and reassurance; Ingrid Brudvig: thank you for your conscientious editing and encouragement; and Andrea Rother: thank you for your personal and professional support. Last, but certainly not least, to my research participants (you know who you are): thank you for your friendship, openness and trust.

The research for this book was funded through the South African National Research Fund (Grant Number: 78765), and additionally by SANPAD, as part of the "Taming the Demons: Configurations of Conviviality, Conflicts and Rights in Mobile and Diverse Communities" project. The opinions expressed in this book are entirely mine, and in no way commit the funders of my research.

Table of Contents

About this Book

This book is based on an ethnographic case study conducted among a group of migrants in Cape Town from Malawi, Zimbabwe and South Africa. The book seeks to understand how migrants overcome structural exclusion by forming and maintaining convivial relationships through the Bay Community Church and how this is facilitated by Information and Communication Technologies (ICTs). Conviviality is not a constant state of relations but a process of balancing intimacy, distance and personal and collective interests. Conviviality exists at the precipice of conflict as a creative process of resolving tensions towards a positive outcome. ICTs are implicated in the negotiation of conviviality. They allow for a negotiation of intimacy and distance; although their functions may facilitate more contact than is desired or further distance those already separated physically. This book interrogates the strict division between 'insiders' and 'outsiders' and highlights that migrants are able to sustain multiple networks and relationships, linking their home and host countries. Despite increasingly strict border control and animosity from host communities, migrants are able to overcome imposed identities such as 'outsider'. They do so by using ICTs such as cell phones and Facebook to emphasise their Christian identity, which is one of the main factors for inclusion in church-based networks. Membership with a mixed denominational church such as the Bay further challenges the notion that migrants stick to themselves. Inclusive communities such as the Bay and everyday desires for conviviality evoke the need to reconsider policies too narrowly articulated around the dichotomisation of 'foreigners' and 'nationals', 'home' and 'away', 'us' and 'them'.

Commendations

"This book provides a healthy balance of empirical description, ethnographic analysis, relevant scholarly discussion, and methodological reflection. The topic is timely, both the focus on migrants and their use of new media, within the context of a newer generation Christian community. Paula Hay chooses her theoretical tools and concepts judiciously, whether habitus, spiritual capital, agency, space, gender, embodiment or transnational networking, rightly interrogating any rigid distinctions between insiders and outsiders or intimacy and distance, for example. She offers some valuable pointers at the end about the challenges and potential of multi-sited fieldwork and the social-scientific study of ICTs. Not surprisingly her heightened reflexivity leads her to hope for a greater democratization of the knowledge production process."

Rosalind I. J. Hackett, Professor of the History of Religions, University of Tennessee, Knoxville, USA

"The analysis and discussions in this study are informed by a sophisticated knowledge and use of the relevant scientific literature. The book demonstrates Paula Hay's ability to present a substantial body of research results concerning the particular nexus made by migration, a low socioeconomic condition, the experience of belonging to a worship community and the efficient use of ICTs. It is worth mentioning that Hay has not relied only on interviews but has also established such interpersonal relationships as to experience the bodily and material conducts of worship and the practical use of ICTs. This experience has prompted an impressive discussion in reflexive anthropology."

Jean-Pierre Warnier, Professor of Anthropology and Material Culture,Centre d'Etudes africaines (EHESS-IRD), Paris, France

Note on the Author

Paula Hay was born in Canada and moved to South Africa in 2009. She completed her high school studies at the United World College of Hong Kong, received her Bachelor of Social Sciences from University College Utrecht in the Netherlands, and holds a Masters in Social Anthropology from the University of Cape Town.

From 2012 to 2014, Paula worked as a research assistant at the Centre for Occupational and Environmental Health Research at the University of Cape Town. There she worked on the development of educational materials for government workers spraying herbicides throughout the Western Cape. Paula organised the Anthropology Southern Africa Conference held at the University of Cape Town in 2012. Between 2009 and 2014, she worked periodically with the Earth Sciences Consultancy Umvoto Africa has a researcher on projects related to community development and disaster risk reduction. Her interest in migrants stems from her own experiences as a foreigner.

Chapter 1

Introduction
Negotiating Intimacy and Distance: Migration, Religion and Information Communication Technology at the Bay Community Church

Research Background

Xenophobia and Belonging

In May 2008, a series of xenophobic attacks erupted in South Africa, leaving at least 60 dead and tens of thousands displaced (Crush 2008: 11; 56). Reports stressed poverty and desperation as underlying causes. The Human Sciences Research Council (HSRC) (2008: 18; 56) cited that foreigners were blamed for a lack of housing, jobs, water and sanitation services as well as for crime and the spread of diseases such as HIV/ AIDS. However, reports such as the HSRC's fell back on labels of 'xenophobic' violence, which prevented analysis as to why 21 of the 62 killed in the attacks were South Africans (Sharp 2008: 2; Duponchel 2013: 2). Attacks on South African nationals suggests that identities and ideas of belonging are historically and socially constructed and exist in a reality that is infiltrated by state power structures and bounded notions of belonging and criteria for citizenship that is different to national identity (Landau 2011).

The extreme wealth divide that many anticipated would lessen after the 1994 democratic elections has remained, if not gotten worse (Landau 2012: 11). During apartheid the state labelled and excluded certain groups from politics and urban spaces. Black Africans from rural areas were labelled as 'foreign natives' who belonged in their designated homelands (Bantustans) but were temporarily allowed into cities as labour (Landau 2012: 5). Thus the concept of the 'nation' was primarily an urban one (Neocosmos 2006: 19); apartheid-era spatial planning and regulation was concerned with protecting privileged insiders and excluding rural, native outsiders who were seen as a threat to stability and health (Landau 2012: 11). Today, the conception of a threat from rural 'others' has been shifted to immigrants who are seen as flooding into South Africa from 'backward' countries and 'failed states'; they are the new "impoverished other", argues Neocosmos (2006: 19). Migrants have become scapegoats for a lack of service delivery, disease, and crime at the official and local levels. Landau contends that from the perspective of poor South Africans "there is no irony in insisting on such overt exclusion as a means of overcoming past discrimination and injustice.

With such logic in place, the post-apartheid state's evident failure at rebirth has generated volatile conditions that initially gave off sparks and, in May 2008, ignited [in xenophobic attacks]." (Landau 2012: 11)

Accounts of the xenophobic attacks might suggest that aggressive identity construction dominates South Africans' relationships with outsiders. However, the mobility of migrants on the margins and the networks they have established indicate a more complex picture of relationships and belonging in South Africa. Migrants have managed their structural exclusion by developing convivial relationships within migrant and local communities (Nyamnjoh 2006: 4). This book focuses on the convivial relationships and social networks forged by migrants at the Bay Community Church

2

in Cape Town and through religious life. Migration is a complex term, given that internal and external migrations both bring into question belonging and the insider or outsider status of those involved. In this book, the migrants of interest are those that have left home for Cape Town out of economic necessity. For the purposes of this book, the term migrant also includes South Africans that have moved to Cape Town from other parts of the country.

An Introduction to the Bay

The Bay Community Church (commonly known as 'the Bay') sits on the outskirts of the stark and gated Capricorn Business Park, just off the M5 Highway on the False Bay Coast, approximately 20km from central Cape Town. They Bay considers itself a non-denominational church but associates itself most closely with the Charismatic movement. [1] The church is juxtaposed against Capricorn Township and the harsh realities of migration in South Africa. All of the migrants that participated in this study reside in Capricorn Township, an area largely comprised of coloured, black and migrant populations, and known for its high levels of drug abuse (particularly the local version of Crystal Meth, known as Tik), gang violence and high unemployment (83%) (LivingHope 2013). Although not all of the migrants from outside of South Africa that I spent time with and interviewed experienced xenophobia on a daily basis, they all cited it as a concern and *"part of the reality of living in South Africa."* [2] In this context, it is notable that the Bay has been referred to as a 'home away from home' by some of its

---

[1] Interview with Sheldon Kidwell at the Bay Community Church (19 July 2012).

[2] Interview with Diana at her home in Capricorn (24 July 2012).

migrant members. The Bay has approximately 450 members, over 50% of which reside in Capricorn and 25% of which are migrants.[3]

The atmosphere at the Bay can be characterised as warm, friendly and convivial; however, I argue that conviviality at the Bay is negotiated by balancing intimacy and distance in relationships between people from a variety of socio-economic and national backgrounds. The negotiation of contradictory feelings of aversion and curiosity at the Bay can result in hostility and animosity as well as an acceptance of difference and a discovery of similarities. Conviviality exists at the edge of conflict. In working out tensions positively and achieving conviviality people avoid going over this precipice. This process is ultimately on-going and depends both on the agency and aspirations of the individuals involved and on ways in which their subjectivity is governed, such as through religious rituals. This book charts migrants' communication configurations and strategies to explore how ICTs are used to navigate church structures and form relationships. ICTs, particularly the cell phone, are implicated in the negotiation of intimacy and distance due to the strategic adoption of the functions provided (e.g. voice call and text messaging).

My overarching research question is: *How do migrants form and maintain convivial relationships at the Bay Community Church and how is this facilitated by the capacities provided by Information Communication Technologies?*

---

[3] Estimates from Sheldon Kidwell, Pastor at the Bay Community Church (interview at the Bay 19 July 2012). Migrants in this case specifically referred to non-South African citizens.

Research Contribution

The data presented in this book is the result of fieldwork conducted between June 2012 and September 2012; and November 2012 and January 2013 My methods included formal and semi-structured interviews, participant observation at church events and services, and 'deep hanging out' (Geertz 1998) with church members in their homes and during their everyday activities.

My research is situated within current anthropological debates on communication, development, technology and society (Castells *et al.* 2007 and Horst and Miller 2006). This research forms part of a larger project, entitled 'Information and Communication Technologies (ICTs), mobility and the reconfiguration of marginality in South Africa'. The aims of this project are to investigate transformations brought about by ICTs, particularly cell phones, among socially marginal groups in South Africa, in this case migrants. The book sets out to consider in what contexts conviviality and conflict emerge between foreign migrants and locals who share spaces in Cape Town and how ICTs engender new configurations of conviviality and/ or conflict. With a more nuanced understanding of these issues, the book may contribute to development agendas and debates surrounding ICTs and African development.

Intimacy, Distance and Conceptualising Conviviality

Luepnitz (2002) conceptualises conviviality as a negotiation of tensions between intimacy and distance. She draws on Freud's interpretation of Schopenhauer's fable about porcupines who try to keep from freezing by huddling together. As they get closer and closer together, they start to poke each other with their quills and must spread out to avoid the pain, thus beginning to shiver again. Freud interpreted the story as a lesson about boundaries in that "no one can tolerate a too intimate approach to his neighbour" (2002: 2). Luepnitz argues that people and communities struggle on a daily basis to "balance privacy and community, concern for self and others..." (2002: 53). She contends that we must allow for implicit feelings of animosity, aversion and hostility in relationships, in addition to love.

Lacan (cited in Luepnitz 2002: 15) emphasises that no one is psychologically whole; the ideal union to which people aspire does not exist. Individuals who assume completeness have no chance of intimacy, as it is only through making someone else inferior that they can attempt to prove their superiority and completeness. In the context of xenophobia, the xenophobe might act as though the foreigner were inferior in order to prove their own superiority. Indeed Landau (2001) emphasises that migrants have been dehumanized and constructed as a threatening, impoverished 'other' flooding in and taking over. Space must be made, Luepnitz argues, for being separate and different.

Agency is important to consider in the context of conviviality as the quest for individual fulfilment may be tempered by collective interests. Agency is often emphasised as being an individual navigation of social structure, but Nyamnjoh (2002: 111) calls for a consideration of inter-subjective agency – "how are individuals able to be who they are through relationships with others?" The group, in that sense, is more than just a composite of many individual interests. Conviviality allows for the empowerment of the individual and group, alike, not marginalisation of one by or for the other. It implies a sense of jovial togetherness, where the individual can express him or herself in a hospitable space but may also have to exercise restraint in order to maintain this merriness (Nyamnjoh 2002). In the context of migration, the idea of inter-subjective agency is useful to consider the reasons that migrants migrate and join a particular church on their arrival. They may move out of an individualistic desire to seek new opportunities but may also be bound by social and familial obligations once they arrive.

Conviviality at the Bay is facilitated by the spontaneous and expressive style of Charismatic worship, which produces a sense of openness and intimacy. Conviviality traditionally implies festive, jovial, merry relations but it has also been defined by Hinchliffe and Whatmore (2006) as the accommodation of difference of human and non-human inhabitants in the context of city life. Overing and Passes (2000) describe the interplay between forces of peace and conflict within Amazonian communities. They contend that the constructive and the destructive are mutually implicated in conviviality. A collective state of tranquillity is the highest achievement for Amazonian people, and conviviality is the process by which friction and forces such as anger and hate are transformed into harmony.

Religion and Information and Communication Technologies

Both religion and ICTs are implicated in the formation of relationships which problematize the strict divisions between 'outsiders' and 'insiders'. Through religion and ICTs migrants create and maintain multiple and heterogeneous networks that are not necessarily geographically or culturally confined.

7

ICTs may also be used to construct and emphasise certain identities through such networks in order to establish a trans-local religious identity over a nationalist one. There is a tendency argues Molony (2007) to see users in the developing world as passive recipients of technologies, rather than active users. As van Binsbergen (2004) argues, there has been an unfortunate focus in the study of ICTs in Africa on what ICTs do to users, rather than what users do with ICTs through processes of social appropriation. With ICTs, migrants are able to connect with kin in other regions, share crucial information, and gain access to resources (see Madianou and Miller 2011; Fonchingong 2010; de Bruijn *et al.*, 2009). However, the cell phone's capacities for instant communication are tempered by the price of airtime and poor connectivity. While migrants may use ICTs to maintain contact with people in their home countries, technology can also facilitate harassment, the maintenance of unwanted connections, and unrealistic demands for money (Nyamnjoh 2005). The possibility to 'call on God' can mediate the tensions of being called upon for support from home. Being devoted to God gives believers the privilege of persuading God to act (Goliama 2011: 169) and ICTs facilitate an immediate connection by allowing users to post prayers on Facebook or send text messages requesting prayers from fellow church members.

Membership at the Bay can provide important bridging and bonding social capital for migrants (Putnam 2000). It can also lead to alternative conceptualisations of kinship. Fellow worshippers can be considered 'brothers and sisters in Christ' (Aasgaard 2004) and are called upon for support when genealogical kin back home are unable or unwilling to support. The expectations associated with kinship via church membership must further be negotiated. The cell phone is implicated in this negotiation because it allows for more or less intimate interactions depending on the situation (e.g. sending a text message vs. voice call).

Chapter Outline

In *Chapter Two: Home and Away: Methods and Ethics in the Context of Multi-Spaces Fieldwork* I describe my research methods, namely participant observation, semi-structured interviews, and 'deep hanging out' (Geertz 1998). Gupta and Ferguson (1997) emphasise that communities are formed in interconnected spaces, which informed my multi-spaces fieldwork. I discuss the 'unbounded' nature of my field sites as well as the physical and social boundaries that required me to negotiate my field throughout fieldwork. This chapter will also describe the ethical issues that arose during fieldwork and the implications for knowledge production. I discuss the difficulties of co-production and accommodating knowledge generated by research participants.

In *Chapter Three: "A home away from home"[4]: Negotiating Capital and Conviviality at the Bay Community Church* I investigate the Bay as a convivial space and a 'home away from home' for its migrant members. I provide a contextual background on the Pentecostal and Charismatic Church movement and a history of the Bay. I draw on Warnier (2006; 2009) to explore the ways in which warmth and intimacy were inscribed on bodies through ritual and expressed in interactions between church members. Space for being both separate and together was facilitated by the 'one Kingdom' identity put forth by the

---

[4] Quote from Diana in reference to the Bay Community Church (17 July 2012); Gregory and Joseph (9 July 2012)

9

church, emphasizing mixing among cultures and religious backgrounds in the presence of Christ. I argue that religion is ultimately a greater criterion for inclusion than other differences such as social and cultural background, but that these differences are negotiated in the context of relationships between individual church members.

In *Chapter Four: Inside and Outside, Intimacy and Distance: Migrants' Use of Information and Communication Technology in the Context of the Bay Community Church*, I argue that migrants use ICTs to form convivial networks and relationships and to negotiate belonging in Cape Town and at the Bay. I argue that ICTs, particularly Facebook, are implicated in migrants' emphasis on their Christian identities in order to belong. I highlight that while technologies allow for the transcendence of certain boundaries they may also impose new boundaries through their use. I draw on de Bruijn *et al.*'s (2009) argument that technology shapes the user just as the user shapes the technology.

In *Chapter Five: Conclusion: A Reflection on Research Findings and Multi-Spaces Anthropological Fieldwork*, I emphasise that migrants' inter-subjective negotiation of belonging in many places brings into question the binary notions of 'insiders' and 'outsiders', 'home' and 'away'. I further conclude that policies that are too focused on narrow conceptions of 'foreigner' and 'national' should be reconsidered in order to take into account convivial relationships between migrants and South Africans. The conclusion also makes recommendations for further academic research on religion and migration and ICTs.

Chapter 2

Home and Away: Methods and Ethics in the Context of Multi-Spaces Fieldwork

Introduction

In this chapter I explore my journey in multi-spaces ethnographic fieldwork conducted between June and September 2012 and November 2012 and January 2013. Fieldwork entailed attending 20 church services; 12 Home Group meetings, seven Fire Starter sessions; two Prayer Furnace (intensive prayer) sessions; and conducting 20 formal interviews; as well as spending time informally with informants. I discuss the 'unbounded' nature of my field spaces and the ways in which physical and socially constructed boundaries between places and people required me to negotiate and re-define my 'field' throughout my fieldwork (Candea 2007: 171). The line between being a researcher and being a friend blurred significantly as I became friends with many of the people involved in my research. I will discuss the nature of these friendships in this chapter as it informed my data collection methods. I will also touch on the ethical issues I encountered in my fieldwork and their implications for knowledge production.

Curiosity, Friendship and Fieldwork

I had five main participants as well as several other members of the Bay Community Church who I interviewed formally or engaged with during the course of fieldwork. Gregory and

Miriam informed me when there were events happening at the church and Joseph, a pious 40-year old man from Malawi, made an effort to involve me in church events that I might have shied away from such as intensive prayer sessions. I also engaged with Diana and Tendai, a couple from Zimbabwe who were my first contacts in the field and who helped me to network with other migrants. Bernard (2006: 152) highlights that those who are cynical about their own culture can be excellent informants. Although not necessarily outcasts, they feel somewhat marginal to or disenchanted with their culture and tend to be observant and reflective insiders. I did not actively seek contact with such informants, but Miriam, a vibrant 30-year old Zulu woman from Mpumalanga living alone in Cape Town, and Lisa a 32-year old Zimbabwean woman dissatisfied by Zimbabwean church networks, proved to be excellent informants precisely because of their willingness to share their criticisms of their networks and environments (see Bernard 2006: 153).

My research methods of participant observation, semi-structured interviews, and 'deep hanging out' (Geertz 1998) brought up questions around friendships in the field and ideas around studying "up" or "down" in anthropology (Nyamnjoh 2012b). Within the first two months of my research, Miriam, Joseph, Gregory and I had been "hanging out" frequently and our conversations arose more and more naturally. To consider them 'participants' in my study seemed to be detached, and an inappropriate label for our relationships. Bernard (2006: 196) writes that during ethnography, one develops "close relationships with a few informants... You can't choose these people. They and you choose each other, over time." Malinowski's (1922) conceptualisation of participant-observation offered a valuable tool for anthropologists to break from typical approaches to fieldwork which involved distancing between ethnographers and subjects (McGee and Warms 2000). Malinowski (1922: 21) claims that in order to gain insights not afforded to an 'outsider' the anthropologist had to "join himself in what is going on," to record the feel and rhythm of everyday life as an active member of the community. (See the excerpt from my field notes Meeting the 'Capricorn Guys' in the text box below).

Meeting the 'Capricorn Guys'

Today (June 27th 2012) was my first Home group meeting. Yesterday I made contact with Diana, the leader of the 'Capricorn Home Group'. She had heard from Sheldon, one of the Pastors at the Bay, that I was coming, and warmly welcomed me to the meeting. I tentatively made my way to Lisa's house at the edge of Capricorn Township where the 'Capricorn guys' (as termed by Sheldon) meet. After the prayer meeting was over, Lisa served tea and I explained my research and the basic concepts around participant observation. Although there seemed to be a positive curiosity about me I felt awkward and wondered how I would approach people and ask to be part of their lives. As I stood up to leave, however, Gregory came to me, smiled curiously, and said, "so when will you come?"... "When will I come to meet with you?" I asked. "Yes" he said, "when will you come?"... "How about next week?" I asked. We exchanged cell phone numbers and my first connection 'in the field' was formed.

In December, several months into my fieldwork, Gregory, a jovial 29-year old man from Malawi, said to me "sometimes I think Paula... imagine I had never gone to that

Home Group meeting. We might not have become friends."[5] Reflecting on my first evening at the Home Group meeting, I deliberated that Gregory had approached me out of curiosity. Perhaps he had ideas of personal material gain but he never implied such desires. When I first went to meet Gregory in early July 2012,[6] his friend Joseph was also visiting. Joseph jumped in on the questions I asked Gregory, delivered long and thoughtful answers and then carried on listening to music with his headphones. On this visit, Miriam entered to charge her phone. I was taken aback by the way she confidently bounded in, said a few words, set her phone up to charge and bounced out the door again. Her familiarity made me realise how much of an outsider I was. Reflecting on that moment provided a good yardstick in terms of my progress in getting to know Miriam, Gregory and Joseph. At my next meeting at Gregory's, Miriam confessed that she had asked Gregory if she could come.[7] Again a curiosity drove another participant to me. Ultimately I did not have to follow a snowball to gather participants, the snowball gathered me.

Anthropological fieldwork is more than just the formation of a research-subject relationship, as it involved the development of friendships. Although I considered friendship to be a voluntary, equal relationship, Paine (1969: 507) contends that the 'emotional content' of friendship can differ greatly between relationships. In conversations with family and friends outside of my research I described my 'participants' as 'church friends'. Friendships must be maintained through trust and loyalty (Beer 2001). Beer (2001)

---

[5] Driving with Gregory and Miriam (16 December 2012).

[6] Informal meeting with Gregory at his home in Capricorn (3 July 2012).

[7] On 9 July 2012.

14

notes, however that sharing and trust as the basis of friendship also means that friendship entails a risk. If the friendship ends, there is the danger that secrets will be shared. As a researcher I was ultimately trying to get information, often confidential. There was necessarily an overlap between the researcher-participant relationship and a friendship because of the levels of trust required. Being in the field and 'deep hanging out' (see Geertz 1998) entailed many of the activities that could build friendship such as sharing stories, keeping in touch via text message, spending time in spaces of mutual interest such as at church gatherings, and exchanging goods and gifts.

Considering my 'participants' as friends obliged me to temper the tendency to romanticise our mutual curiosity. Gregory put a picture on Facebook of the two of us and labelled it 'we r gud friends' and commented that he had missed me recently at church.[8] When I saw it I was flattered and proud of being recognised by Gregory as a friend. I also wondered if the picture was part of his construction of a Cape Town identity to show friends in Malawi. That being said, my activities on Facebook also constituted identity construction (Zhao *et al.* 2008) and as I 'liked' the photo, I was complicit in this activity.

Being good friends and constructing an identity around this friendship were not necessarily mutually exclusive. When Miriam asked me to pick her up from the hospital in October 2012 after an operation she was having, I felt it was my duty as a 'friend' with a car to do so. I felt I had accomplished what I had set out to do through fieldwork –build relationships. However, it was also possible that my eagerness to develop relationships made me more amenable to

---

[8] Posted on Facebook (9 January 2013).

exploitation. Indeed tensions around giving and reciprocity are negotiated in the context of friendship and calls for a greater recognition of the inter-subjective nature of relationships in the field. Ultimately Miriam was much more than just an 'informant' to me and I was more than just a 'researcher' to her –both of us were capable of manipulation as well as kindness and friendship.

Owen (2011) captures the complexity of research-subject relationships in her work with Congolese migrants in Muizenberg. Owen considers the complexity of her 'nativeness' to the area (having grown up only 20 minutes away) and her 'marginal' position as a coloured woman studying the non-native, alien refugee in her own home space. She describes convivial and intimate relationships that form in moving between subject positions and the overcoming of power dynamics between the 'researcher' and 'researched'. Conviviality for the researcher and his or her subjects is a form of agency in that sense; the ability to work out tensions and establish relationships that move beyond commonly divisive categories.

My Multiple Field Spaces

Although I remained in Cape Town throughout my fieldwork, my interactions were not limited to physical places but also took place in virtual spaces (e.g. online and cell phone communication). Given that I remained in Cape Town, my fieldwork is not characterised as multi-sited but multi-spaced, as I worked in multiple locations across Cape Town and virtually.

My fieldwork was informal in many ways. Although I formally arranged meetings and interviews early in my

16

fieldwork in July and August 2012, many encounters occurred because I was invited to spend time with someone, or during Home Group bible study and Sunday services. I made an effort to accompany and assist people with their regular activities such as grocery shopping after church on a Sunday or driving people home after Home Group and Fire Starter meetings. People's curiosity often came out in these informal moments and I sometimes ended up answering more questions about myself. Teaching Gregory and Miriam to drive (over the course of seven Sundays) proved invaluable in terms of getting to know them as friends and provided a safe space in which we could engage in mutually personal discussion.

It was also interesting for me to engage with participants in locations that were familiar to me but less familiar to them such as the wealthier suburb of Kalk Bay where my family stays. Joseph mentioned that these experiences gave him a better understanding of my life, possibly serving to blur the researcher-subject line. By spending time with the migrants in their homes, I observed their use of ICTs as well as their reactions to feeling included or excluded from church events, which complemented direct interviews.

In my fourth week of fieldwork on July 4th 2012, Fire Starters began. Fire Starters was a course developed to bring all of the Home Groups together to discuss basic principles of Christian faith and provide guidance for followers to deepen their faith.[9] During Fire Starters, prayer and bible study took place and a short motivational sermon was

---

[9] Fire starters was a 12-week course with three sessions of four weeks, with two two-week breaks in between. The course ran from July 4th to July 25th 2012; August 15th to September 5th 2012; and September 26th to October 17th 2012.

delivered. Individual members were invited to prophesise for other members (giving them encouragement with regards to a current situation or future prospects) or give testimonies on the positive work of God in their lives. People frequently asked questions on how to sustain their faith and the nature of God. Witnessing these activities was important in terms of understanding how people reinforce and negotiate their identities as Christians.

Participating in Fire Starters also placed me in the field as a researcher and an active course participant. Sheldon, a leader at the Bay, told me in after Fire Starters on August 22nd 2012, "I will use you as an example as what it means to get involved in the life of a church. You just got in there [at Fire Starters]! It's great to see." Diana introduced me to the Capricorn Fire Starters Group as a new member of the church and a researcher, assigning me to both positions without rendering them mutually exclusive. Although I continued to feel like an outsider in terms of my spiritual beliefs, I also engaged with Fire Starters as a participant, doing the homework exercises and engaging in discussions around religious texts, as well as being part of group coordination such as collecting and dropping off of members of the Fire Starters group.

Negotiating the Familiar and Unfamiliar

While the idea of the 'field' in anthropology evokes images of a faraway, exotic space, to which anthropologists had to travel for months to get to (Gupta and Ferguson 1997: 8), this image no longer applies. It is arguable that even small scale societies were never as geographically and culturally bounded as they were conceived to be by early anthropologists. In the context of a mobile, changing, and globalising world, the increasingly blurring lines between 'here', 'there'; centre and periphery, render that view even more obsolete. In conducting fieldwork with multiple field spaces, many of which I considered familiar at the start of my fieldwork, I noted that physical proximity does not necessarily eliminate social and emotional barriers or differences. Fieldwork can occur in spaces that exist side by side by connecting places, spaces and people that might otherwise not associate.

Discovering that close family friends of mine also attended the Bay reflected some of Gupta and Ferguson's (1997: 302) ideas around the blurry line between home and away, "insider" and "outsider". Gupta and Ferguson call on researchers not to assume discontinuity and autonomy in spaces but consider how communities are formed in interconnected spaces characterised by profound "bifocality" (1997: 36), or perhaps rather multifocality (Nyamnjoh 2012a). Having family friends in the field made me not just a researcher but a member of a wider network. This close familiarity with members of the church and the warmth of the people at the Bay was juxtaposed for me against the foreignness of participating in new religious activities and feeling unable to disclose my spiritual beliefs candidly.

Feelings of familiarity and unfamiliarity were relevant for understanding the experiences of the migrants that I worked with throughout my fieldwork. Fieldwork is central to anthropological work precisely because it provides an opportunity for inter-subjective encounters and experiences from which the anthropologist can build an understanding of meaning-making amongst a particular group. Geertz (1973: 27) emphasises the importance of "thick description" as the object of ethnography, arising out of finding one's feet in the field and a personal experience which one tries to analyse and formulate theoretically.

My fieldwork in Capricorn also led me to reflect on ways in which ICTs are implicated in a negotiation of the familiar and unfamiliar. When I first started travelling to Capricorn on week day evenings to meet informants, I struggled to navigate the space, often in the dark (see the excerpt from my field notes 'Finding Gregory' in the text box below).

Finding Gregory

Tonight (July 19th, 2012) was a cold drizzling evening. I was on my way to Gregory's place in Capricorn Township when I made a wrong turn and found myself weaving my car confusedly along muddy roads through rows and rows of houses and crowds of people coming home from work. People looked at me as though they knew I was lost and moved reluctantly out of the way of my car –a frustrating reminder that I did not belong. I clung to my phone for security. It has no GPS function and calling Gregory would not have aided me as I had no landmarks to indicate where I was. Yet the idea that Gregory was just a call away made him seem physically close. In a moment of total disconnect with my physical space –connection was possible in an instant. I somehow imagined that with a phone I was safe no matter what. That being said, when I called Gregory again for directions I struggled to hear and understand him. I wondered if technology had in fact created the problem in the first place. We hadn't agreed on a more accessible meeting place beforehand because I could 'just call when I was close' and I had relied on his directions over the phone to know where to go. In that sense technologies might provide both distance and connection and be enabling and disabling at the same time. When I managed to get to a main road and called Gregory again for directions (and was able to understand them) I felt found.

In the space of a short evening my cell phone provided me with security and facilitated both frustrating and relieving communication. In my fearful state I worried that it might make me the target of robbery but I also clung to it for security, assuming that I was safe with it in my hand. As an 'outsider' to the area, my cell phone was my way to be found, but at the same time may have been the cause of a lack of direct communication prior to meeting. The experience highlighted the ways in which dependency on the cell phone can be both enabling and disabling. My experience of getting lost also highlighted that the 'insider's' (i.e. Gregory's) privileged knowledge should not be taken for granted. Although Gregory was considered by many in Capricorn to be an outsider, in my terms he was very much an insider. This would further indicate that being an insider for Gregory and for me as an anthropologist was relational and something which had to be constantly negotiated.

The experience of getting lost in the field literally, was reflective of the wider fieldwork experience in that one's insider-outsider status is not fixed but constantly negotiated depending on the situation, unique habitus (Bourdieu 1990), and material tools such as the cell phone, that one can draw on. Habitus (Bourdieu 1990) refers to socialised norms and dispositions obtained through upbringing or training which guide the way agents interact in particular fields. Tendencies and dispositions are shaped by past events and inform current practices and perceptions (Bourdieu 1984: 170). However, one may be required to shift one's habitus in relation to new contexts, or draw on one's habitus to negotiate structures. Habitus is not solely a result of agency or structure but an interplay between the two over time (Bourdieu 1990: 56). In the context of the 'anthropological field' the anthropologist may draw on their training and socialised norms unconsciously, but may also have to improvise and change dispositions in order to adapt to new fields (see Wacquant 2005: 316).

Studying "Up", "Down" and "Around"

The idea of the unfamiliar can be very enticing to an anthropologist. Indeed I initially planned to conduct my research in a predominantly 'migrant' church –one in which most of the members of the church were migrants and possibly a more marginal church existing in a township. This idea was alluring, but I was reflective of the tendency of anthropologists to opt for what they considered to be 'exotic' field sites. I considered this in the context of Nyamnjoh's (2012b: 70) criticism of a tendency among South African anthropologists to "study down" to those considered marginal and disenfranchised, but rarely horizontally or "up" to the privileged and ruling elites. Indeed, this trend is evidenced by the terms of my project, which is a study of those considered to be on the 'margins'.

I ultimately selected a field site because of the diversity of the congregation. In exploring conviviality, it seemed highly relevant to work in a setting in which people come from a variety of socio-economic backgrounds and draw on a range of cultural logics in order to belong and form convivial relationships. Gordon (2013: 5) emphasises in his response to Nyamnjoh's (2012b) article to beware of falling into a trap of essentialising groups with categories such as "up" or "down" in favour of studying people's interactions "around". Gordon writes (2013: 5): "I simultaneously strive to study up and down and reflect on how I am influenced by and subject to my research projects."

Although I spent most of my 'deep hanging out' (Geertz 1998) time with a few migrants living in different areas of Capricorn, I also spent time with members of the church that could be classified as white middle class. Anthropology, as emphasised by Geertz (1973) is a study of behaviour and social action –how claims made by social actors play out in particular social contexts. The task of the anthropologist is to uncover the hierarchy of meaning in which behaviours are enacted, perceived and interpreted. Considering the claim made by migrants that the church is a home away from home, or the claim made by church leaders that the church reflects the 'one Kingdom' ideal, participating in conversations and activities with a variety of church members was important in order to consider how idealistic and religious notions of conviviality play out amongst church members that exist in a range of contexts in everyday life.

Reflexivity as a Lifelong Process[10] : Ethics and Implications for Knowledge Production

Considering ethics in the field, Malkki's (2007) assertion that fieldwork is a form of 'improvisation' is particularly useful. The anthropologist cannot be considered a neutral bystander but "takes up social space as a person" (2007:177) and must draw on both instinct, emotional intelligence, and an academic and ethnical compass in new interactions and situations. As a social person in the field, one of my dominant reservations was misrepresentation. By participating in religious rituals I ultimately represented myself to the wider community as a Christian and internally I struggled with the precarious balance between being true to myself, exploring personal esoteric matters in the field, and also achieving participant observation. I was honest when people queried as to whether I was a Christian and was sincere with my participants with regards to my personal, spiritual experiences

---

[10] Nyamnjoh 2012b: 81.

and explorations at the Bay. Yet I was caught off guard a few times. When a young man at the church asked me if I was a Christian and then inserted accusingly, "You're not just here for the research, right?"[11] I fumbled. I often felt that my nebulous responses regarding my spiritual beliefs were not satisfactory for steadfast believers and was sometimes overwhelmed by abruptly feeling dismissed or unwelcome. However, I was also often surprised by the kind words I received and insight into the Charismatic church that I was able to gain as an honest outsider. Speaking to a leader in the church I received the following response to my comment that I struggle with the dogmatic nature of religion: "Hey I don't like religion either. I hated it as a child and rebelled against it at some point. Here we have tried to break from the legalistic part of religion. Do this or that so God will love you. It's about what's in your heart."[12]

In a small community such as the Bay, privacy was one of my primary ethical concerns. I have used pseudonyms throughout this work. As I formed friendships in the field, data gathering often occurred in the context of casual discussions as well as informal virtual interactions such as text messages and phone calls. I always asked if I could use virtual interactions as part of my research but it was more practical to verify ideas and conclusions as they emerged.

Writing about religion, I have been especially concerned about the ethical implications of reducing people's tangible religious experiences to academic theories. Joseph, a dignified devoted Christian, did not fully approve of my consideration that religious experiences might be derived from certain types of kinesthetic movements. To him they are purely the Holy

---

[11] During tea break after a Sunday church service (5 August 2012).
[12] During tea break after a Sunday church service (12 August 2012).

Spirit. I have tried to pay attention to the effects of religious experiences rather than trying to expound them. Being aware of Adichie's (2009) warning against the 'danger of a single story', however, I fear I have failed to engage in co-production and avoid taking advantage of informants' input without acknowledging them. Ultimately what is reflected here is still my story, my experiences and my reflections, even as I have sought to be as compassionate and sympathetic to the perceptions and interpretations of my interlocutors as possible.

The difficulties of democratising knowledge production are addressed by Bourdieu (2004: 6). He proposes that the production of knowledge within a particular discipline is legitimated by rules and norms adopted by the discipline itself. These norms are reinforced and reproduced through a system that rewards whichever knowledge best demonstrates and corroborates the accepted 'truth' of that discipline. This speaks to Appadurai's (2000: 19) claim that in order to talk about and contest dominant theories of globalisation, one has to already be part of that conversation, and therefore to be cognizant of the vocabulary used. The anthropologist therefore faces a challenge in terms of how to accommodate knowledge generated by research 'participants'. Appadurai (2000) suggests that a solution may be found in increased dialogue, greater reflexivity and better accountability. Reflexivity entails incorporating within anthropological theorising "a critique of its own locations, positions and interests" (Moore, 1999: 9).

Showing participants sections of my work has required me to consider the role of conflict in co-production. For example, when I showed Gregory some of my field notes, his concern was about how he would be seen as opposed to the accuracy of the moment I described or how it fit into the broader research question. Gregory jested that he did not like the way he sounded in a section of my field notes.[13] Although his concern with how he was portrayed was interesting in and of itself, I still had to explain that it was what he said that was important and tried to ease his fears. Gregory agreed that it was fine but I was left with the feeling that my portrayal of him had not been co-produced or co-interpreted in any way. Considering ideas around conviviality, it is arguable that conflict is an important ingredient in the process of knowledge production as it allows for contestations and alternative viewpoints to come to the fore (Nyamnjoh 2012b). I have been eased by Nyamnjoh's (2012b: 81) emphasis that "knowing is a lifelong commitment to reflexivity" and dialogue, especially if anthropology is to recognise temporality and transformation. This process revealed that claims to truth are subject to revision, by both researcher and 'subject'.

Conclusion

In exploring conviviality I felt it was important to select a church in which people draw on a range of cultural logics in order to form convivial relationships. Initially my methods included formal and semi-structured interviews, participant observation at church events and services, and 'deep hanging out' with church members in their homes and during their everyday lives. Joining Fire Starters, the Home Group course offered by the church, I became part of the coordination of

---

[13] Meeting with Gregory at McDonalds in Capricorn Business Park (17 January 2013).

the 'Capricorn Group' and was able to engage both as a researcher and participant.

I engaged with my informants in locations that were more familiar to me, which I believe served to obscure the researcher-subject line as my informants were able to encounter my social worlds. Blurring the researcher-subject line also involved becoming friends with my informants and called into question the inter-subjective nature of relationships in the field. Research entailed many of the activities that build friendships such as sharing stories, exchanging gifts and having fun. In this context, I was compelled to temper my romantic notions of my friendships in the field and, as with other friendships, negotiate tensions around giving, reciprocity, kindness and manipulation.

Moving beyond potentially divisive categories such as 'researcher' and 'researched' entailed moving together between subject positions (e.g. insider and outsider) and between the familiar and unfamiliar. Being an insider or outsider are not fixed categories but are constantly negotiated depending on the social field and unique habitus (Bourdieu 1990) one can employ. As part of my fieldwork experience, feelings of familiarity and unfamiliarity were important in understanding the experiences of the migrants that I worked with.

My main concerns and considerations during this research included anonymity, being honest about not being Christian, and engaging in co-production. Sharing my ideas with my informants throughout the research process was useful for engaging in conversation and eliciting more nuanced or divergent reflections to those initially offered. I felt that I predominantly determined the terms and conditions for participation and production, however I have sought to be as sensitive to the interpretations and opinions of my informants as possible. Incorporating contradictions was important as it allowed for multiple perspectives to be delivered and a negotiation of understanding that privileged inter-subjectivity and conviviality (Nyamnjoh 2012b: 13), the very focus of this book.

Chapter 3

"Home Away From Home": Negotiating Capital and Conviviality at the Bay Community Church

Introduction

The Bay Community Church has been referred to as a 'home away from home' by some of its migrant members and can be considered a space of conviviality. In broad terms it is the merry, jovial and warm atmosphere that makes the Bay a convivial space, facilitated by the particular style of Charismatic worship, which governs bodies towards a logic of open oneness and intimate interactions. Outside of worship, the church is also the site of transnational and local networks which many migrants draw on for social and spiritual capital and to negotiate belonging in a frequently hostile environment. The different habituses (Bourdieu 1990) and values attributed to relationships and networks must be negotiated between members in order to maintain the conviviality that characterises the Bay. I argue that conviviality is not a constant state of relations but a process of building and remaking relationships in order to achieve a balance between intimacy and distance.

Convivial Bodies

It is difficult to define and generalise Pentecostalism as it has a wide variety of doctrines, ritual, organizations, and localised forms of worship.[14] Indeed it is arguably this variability and adaptability to local contexts that has allowed Pentecostalism to establish its global reach with such a variety of manifestations (Anderson 2004: 240). Generally speaking, Pentecostal churches emphasise the immediate presence of God, signs of interventions from God (termed 'gifts of the spirit'), and encourage free and spontaneous expression in worship (Anderson 2004).[15]

The Pentecostal movement traces its roots to 1906, at the Azusa Street mission in Los Angeles, California, a Methodist-sponsored revival. It was there that people claimed to have been "baptized in the Holy Spirit" in the manner recorded in Acts Chapter 2 during the celebration of Pentecost, including speaking in tongues and spontaneous outbursts of emotion (Anderson 2004: 168). The Azusa Street Revival was led by a captivating African American preacher named William Seymour. His congregation was a notorious racial and gender mix uncharacteristic of the time. The people who attended those meetings spread their enthusiasm throughout the United States, and by the early 1970s, the movement had spread to Europe (Anderson 2004: 271). The Charismatic movement is an interdenominational Christian renewal movement and is one of the most popular and fastest-growing forces within the Christian world today. Charismatic churches began to distinguish themselves in the 1960s when

---

[14] Pentecostalism is used here as an all-embracing term for Pentecostal, Charismatic and neo-Charismatic churches.

[15] The evidence for being filled with the Holy Spirit is speaking in tongues. A key difference between Charismatic and Pentecostal doctrine, however, is that Pentecostal groups have largely made speaking in tongues a requirement for and sign of salvation. Conversely, Charismatic groups believe that speaking in tongues is experienced sometime after conversion as long as a person has chosen to be baptised (Anderson 2004).

'gifts of the spirit' became associated with congregations that had previously been considered mainstream and against such manifestations of the Holy Spirit (Anderson 2004: 25) The Charismatic movement advocated that those influenced by Pentecostal tenets, particularly Protestant denominations, could also remain in their chosen denominations (Menzies and Menzies 2000: 38-9). The movement spread to other churches, where clergy began to announce their Pentecostal experiences and held prayer and healing meetings where the sick were prayed for.[16]

I contend that the Pentecostal and Charismatic styles of worship and particularly the style of worship at the Bay facilitate convivial interactions between members. This serves as an important backdrop for the 'bonding capital' (Putnam 2000) that I argue the Bay provides.

---

[16] The charismatic movement spread further within evangelicalism around 1985, termed the Third Wave of the Holy Spirit. The Third Wave has led to the formation of separate churches referred to as "neo-charismatic" organizations (see Burgess *et al.* 2010; Anderson 2004).

A Service at the Bay

As I enter the main hall at 9:30 am, I watch in awe as hundreds of people of different races and socio-economic backgrounds, armed with prayer books and young children, stream in. The church band plays upbeat rock music from the hall stage with the lyrics projected on two large screens facing the congregation. The songs express gratitude for God's grace and for the sacrifice Jesus made for those who believe in Him. Church members greet each other, hug, laugh, sing along and sway to the music, dance, jump for joy, close their eyes, and raise their hands in prayer. The atmosphere is jovial, lively and purposeful. A burst of one person's laughter erupts from across the room and continues for several minutes enticing others to laugh as well. As the last song finishes, a voice on the microphone from someone at the front of the service describes what she feels God wants to say to the congregation: "God knows you and wants the best for you". Pastor Jeff Kidwell, wearing faded blue jeans and an un-tucked dress shirt, jests with members of the audience like a professional comedian, drawing on humorous examples of God's work and Jesus' love in everyday life. His sermon is punctuated by enthusiastic shouts of "amen" and "hallelujah". After the sermon Jeff encourages people to lay hands on each other to pray for certain afflictions. Members crowd around an afflicted individual, touching them with purpose and love. The hall is filled with the quiet hum of prayer and people speaking in tongues.

My first attendance of a Sunday Service at the Bay was on June 17th 2012 (see excerpt from my field notes 'A Service at the Bay' in the text box above). At this first service, I felt awkward and stiff. I stood rigidly at the back of the church and watched the bodies in front of me move freely. As an outsider to religion in general and to the Bay in particular, it was apparent to me that I had to learn certain behaviours and to conduct my body in a certain fashion in order to 'fit in' and in order to engage in 'participant observation' to its fullest extent. Despite the emphasis at the Bay on free expression during worship, I felt that my body needed to be governed in order to fit in, even if only to become more spontaneous. Engaging my body, however awkwardly at first, in singing, dance and touch stimulated an inner joy that I could not ignore and after a few Sundays I was compelled to sing along and move my body. Ross posits that difference in understanding space lies not in culture but in a familiarity and sense of internal rhythm and becoming "patterned" (Al Alvarez 2005: 58 cited in Ross 2010: 70).

Conviviality at the Bay is expressed in physical interactions and bodily practises. There is a great deal of intimacy expressed in the church hall – hugging, warm greetings, and spontaneous prayer by laying hands on people. Inhibitions seem unencumbered and I have certainly felt my heart open. Pentecostals and Charismatics emphasise spontaneity and heartfelt expression and consider ritual to be restrictive, legalistic and disingenuous expression of worship (Anderson *et al.* 2010: 164). Sheldon, Pastor Jeff's son, told me adamantly that it is not ritual, *"just worship"*.[17] Indeed worship at the Bay is considerably informal. However, worship is not unceremonious. The order in which events take place in the course of a service, the type of music played

---

[17] Interview with Sheldon Kidwell at the Bay Community Church (19 July 2012).

and the type of worship encouraged in the church (e.g. speaking in tongues, free expression and movement) all serve to govern bodies towards a particular experience of the divine.

In order to deal with Charismatic ritual, Lindhardt (2011: 9) argues, scholars have had to allow for a collapse of dichotomies – those between spontaneity and control, informality and formality, immediacy and structure. Comaroff and Comaroff (1993: xviii-xix) contend that ritual is not necessarily structured to maintain a system but can allow for actions outside of the boundaries of the ritual itself. Lindhardt (2011: 10) notes that scholars are beginning to focus increasingly on embodied experiences of divinity or a holy presence. These are considered to be an effect of rituals (loosely termed) that involve a mobilisation of the senses kinaesthetically and rhythmically such as when dancing, swaying, singing and praying. Czikszentmihalyi (see Neitz and Spickhard 1990; Lindhardt 2011) has documented the concept of "flow experience" in which experiences of oneness, or holiness, may appear during activities that require a high degree of extreme focus and consciousness such as rock climbing or listening to music.

Bodies at the Bay are governed through ritual towards more convivial and spontaneously intimate interactions with fellow worshippers. As Lindhardt (2011: 3) highlights, rituals serve to formalise moral truths and emphasise collective identities over and above individual intentions. Drawing on Foucault's work on how power is directed at the body (1975, 2001 cited in Warnier 2009: 418; 2006: 188), Warnier emphasises that power is achieved when subjects act seemingly upon their own desire and will, govern their own bodies, and even act upon other subjects. The aim of ritual may be to induce particular spiritual acts (e.g. producing rain or bringing the Holy Spirit into one's being), however it also involves a shaping of the subject. Considering ritual in such a light, it is possible to overcome divides between "subject and object, material culture and the body, technology and magic, religion or ritual." (Warnier 2009: 420).

People, as subjects, are shaped and identified as containers through "routinely incorporated motions, emotions and perceptions" (Warnier 2006: 191) which are also part of a construction of broader technologies of power in the context of social life. In the religious context, the body in Warnier's (2006) terms is the container of the Holy Spirit, and church worship evokes an opening to the Holy Spirit and a closing out of the devil. Bodies channel Christ through speech (prophecies) and healing power (laying hands on afflicted worshippers). At the Bay, techniques of the body are performed in order to lead people into the presence of God and so that worshippers identify themselves as vessels for God to work through. Relationships between worshippers are shaped by this identification with and incorporation of Jesus into the body container. Indeed Warnier's (2009: 419) very definition of "sensori-motor conduct" refers to any bodily motion involving a perceptive activity – including singing, playing music, or kneeling down to pray as subjectivities are shaped and transformed by these practises.

Rituals are part of a mediation of power and agency (Warnier 2006: 419), as the intimacy that is expressed during worship may change or have to be negotiated outside of worship. While conviviality implies a merry, jovial atmosphere, such as at a party, there is always the chance that someone will over extend the intimacy expressed in worship outside of the church context. For example, a church member was asked to leave when it was discovered he was making sexual advances on a young female church member. Conviviality in this sense is both inscribed on the body through ritual as well as negotiated via agency.

The Transnational Bay

This section highlights that Pentecostalism in Africa has networked itself internationally. I draw on theories of transnationalism and spiritual capital to understand some of the ways in which migrants at the Bay draw on networks and their Christian habitus to negotiate belonging and conviviality. Migrants are able to belong at the Bay due to their Christian habitus. However, differences in habitus may also require a negotiation in the church context in order to maintain conviviality.

Transnational Pentecostal Networks

Pentecostalism has been active in Africa since 1970, when missionaries from the Azusa Street Revival in the United States arrived in Liberia and Angola. In Nigeria and Ghana, several churches linked with the Apostolic Church in Britain have grown into enormous organisations (Anderson 2004: 104). In 2000 more than half of Zimbabwe's population belonged to African Pentecostal churches, almost half of South Africa's and over a third of Kenya's population (Anderson 2004: 104). Anderson (2004: 162) claims that Pentecostalism in Africa appeals to a new generation of mobile Africans especially as prominent preachers place high value on internationalism, doing missionary work, and international conventions. The emphasis on transnational religious ties has implications for migrant networks and the capital they can acquire.

The Christ Embassy, started by Nigerian Pastor Christian Oyakhilome (known popularly as Pastor Chris), is a prime example of the reach that African Pentecostalism has had globally. The Christ Embassy has head offices and ministries worldwide. In 2003 Pastor Chris pioneered the first 24 hour Christian Network from Africa to the rest of the world, called LoveWorld (Pastor Chris Online). On most of my visits to Lisa, Joseph and Gregory, I found the LoveWorld channel playing on television in the background, featuring Pastor Chris or another preacher. Lisa and Gregory both subscribe specifically to this channel. The use of television allows religious organisations such as Christ Embassy to work transnationally and connect audiences in multiple places. It also allows migrants such as Lisa and Gregory to participate in religious services and connect with familiar forms of worship and religious leaders even when they are not physically present (Levitt 2002). On Sunday December 2, 2012, I accompanied Miriam and Joseph to the Good Hope Centre in Cape Town where Pastor Karen Victor, a white Afrikaans woman from a South African Christ Embassy Branch led the 'Super Sunday' event. Pastor Karen preached to thousands of Christ Embassy followers, mostly black Africans coming from across Africa and particularly Zimbabwe. Miriam and Joseph knew several people at the event. Although they said their main purpose there was to worship, Joseph noted that such large organisations provide assistance to migrants, such as skills advancement programs or guidance with resume writing. The large scale event was an indication of the transnational reach, popularity, and bridging capacity of Pentecostal movements.

The Bay is linked most closely with a large and fast growing Charismatic movement originating in Britain called New Frontiers, which has over 700 churches in every region of the world. By 1982 there were approximately 100,000 Charismatic churches in Britain with major networks such as New Frontiers and the Vineyard (Anderson 2004: 104). Many of the migrants at the Bay are linked with Christ Embassy and Assemblies of God in their home countries and in Cape Town. This is in line with transnational migration as defined by Glick-Schiller *et al.* (1995: 48) as: "The process by which immigrants forge and sustain simultaneous multi-stranded social relations that link together their societies of origin and settlement." This situates the Bay in transnational networks as an internationally linked organisation and through its individual members. Migrants at the Bay who are connected to religious activities in their home country are part of a bridging of global-local divides and create what Mahler and Hansing (2005: 131) term "the transnationalism of the middle".

I accompanied Miriam and Joseph when they attended religious services outside of the Bay. We attended a service at the large internationally networked church, Christ Embassy in Muizenberg[18] and a small local church in Lavender Hill.[19] Their regular attendance at other churches was important to observe and participate in, in terms of understanding belonging at the Bay as well as belonging to a wider Christian network and community. Focusing on church members' networks gave me some insight into the many types of

---

[18] Beach side suburb of Cape Town (20 January).
[19] Part of the Cape Flats area of Cape Town, notorious for gang violence and drugs (25 November).

relationships that form at and through Bay and the way ICTs are implicated in the negotiation of these relationships.

Networks provided a useful framework from which to explore inter-subjective relationships. As opposed to other categories used to distinguish groups of people (e.g. socio-economic status, language or race), networks, as defined in actor-network theory (ANT) by Callon (1991) and Latour (2005: 25), are not fixed categories but processes, performed by the actors out of which they are developed. Latour (2005: 65) and Callon (1991: 143) use the term "translation" to refer to the ways in which networks stabilise as actors construct common meanings and definitions and form inter-subjective relationships in the pursuit of both individual and collective goals. While ANT advocates an open-ended performance by social actors in a specific field or network (Latour 2005), political realities can serve to confine social actors to particular positions in a network, requiring negotiation. Identities are inherently political in that they are formed by categorising and often excluding outsiders (Delanty 2000). Although identities can be constructed with the creative agency of the actors involved, they are also imposed and deployed in the context of power relations and social or structural locations (Jenkins 1996), which can serve to limit actors' agency in a network.

Negotiating Transnational Belonging

In this section I describe the types of capital that migrants tap into through church membership. I further highlight the ways in which tapping into social capital is implicated in the negotiation of conviviality. On a Wednesday evening before a church event, I joined Diana and Tendai for dinner. I asked

Diana if she experienced xenophobia and if she had ever experienced it at the Bay:

> *"Well it has gotten better but I still hear people in the taxis saying makwerekwere under their breath if I am talking on the phone in Shona. After the violence in 2008 I heard people, many people, saying it's good that they burnt those foreigners. They don't know I can understand Xhosa so I hear the things people say. But at the Bay, ok maybe sometimes someone is unfriendly, but I never feel unwelcome.... Even though Zimbabwe is our home, the Bay is also like home now... It is a home away from home."* [20]

In the context of migration and negotiating belonging in a hostile environment, the description by many of the migrants involved of the Bay as a 'home away from home'[21] is important to take note of. Church membership can have a variety of effects on migrants' relationships with their host and home communities. Churches can provide forms of social and cultural capital (Bourdieu 1990), spiritual capital (Verter 2003), and bonding and bridging capital (Putnam 2000). In this section I argue that migrants construct and draw on church based networks for social and spiritual capital in order to negotiate their outsider status and their independence. I further argue that this is a process of inter-subjective negotiation.

Individual Salvation and Rupture

Meyer (1998: 320; 324) describes the emphasis in Pentecostalism in Ghana on individual salvation, highlighting

---

[20] Interview with Diana at her home in Capricorn (24 July 2012).

[21] The Bay was also described as a 'home away from home' by Gregory and Joseph (9 July 2012).

that many of the adherents to Pentecostalism in Ghana are single or divorced women. With few people to rely on and striving to move upward socio-economically, these women are largely excluded from primarily male-dominated power structures. Miriam, a fiercely independent young woman (determined to get her driver's licence, despite having no access to a car) was eager to move away from extended family in search of a change, and achieve financial and social independence after her mother's death. Miriam was first attracted to Christianity while she was living alone in Cape Town. She told me "I am not alone when I am with Jesus. He knows me and I can do anything. You just have to believe and pray."[22] As Meyer (1998: 320) contends, the Pentecostal church offers an individualist ethic which can correspond with personal aspirations to overcome age, origin and gender.

Pentecostal churches also view poverty and other conditions such as sickness to be associated with sin, as opposed to a socio-economic condition (Anderson 2004: 199). Blessing the Lord is meant to materialise in prosperity. At the Bay, a lack of material wealth is not seen as a sin per se but there is an emphasis that God wants people to prosper. Various forms of wealth were praised and prayers were given for promotions and financial success during services. Gregory spoke often about God in reference to his financial situation and emphasised God's faith in his ability to prosper financially. For example, I received the following text message from Gregory:

"Paula I am very fine but just that I am so busy going up and down looking for money so that she (his wife in Malawi) can be here

---

[22] Interview with Miriam at her home in Capricorn (7 August 2012).

next month. But GOD is faithful I will make it. I hope everything is doing great with you as well?[23]

Meyer's work particularly emphasises rupture from the past as a pre-requisite to joining the church and focuses on deliverance as a central aspect of this rupture. At the individual level, pressures to participate in family rituals can be difficult to overcome. Many of Gregory's family members have reconciled their Christian beliefs with their traditional practises and although he disagrees he tends to "go-along" with rituals at home to avoid being contentious.

Miriam described the tension over participating in traditional practises when she goes home:

> *"I am not comfortable with it but I try to tell them as much as possible about Jesus... Only my brother knows Jesus so he understands... They don't mind that I tell them but they continue to do their traditional practises so I must just watch and be patient."*[24]

While Miriam tries to convert her family and still looks forward to attending family gatherings, her independence is also reinforced by her different religious views and subsequent exclusion from traditional practises. Increased separation from traditional family life may emerge as people emphasise their Christian identity. In this context, viewing the church as a 'home' becomes more important.

---

[23] Original text message: Paula I m very fine but just that I m so busy goin up n down looking fr money so that she can b hr nxt mnth. Bt GOD is faithful I will make it. I hope evrthn is doin great wit u as well? (8 November 2012).

[24] Interview with Gregory and Miriam in Kalk Bay (8 September 2012).

Belonging at the Bay

While some migrants identify more with their home society, Glick Schiller *et al.* (2006) contend that the majority will maintain several identities in order to belong and adapt to precarious living conditions, as well as to be linked to more than one nation. In fact migrants negotiate many worlds as individuals. Kopytoff (1987:11) views the frontier not in its geographical terms as a sparse and undiscovered space, but as a space in which new societies arise out of old ones. Kopytoff's (1987) notion of the frontier also implies a collision of societies. Groups are produced at the frontier when people who are alienated in some way from wider society or the 'metropole' (Kopytoff 1987: 16) distance themselves and unite. Although migrants are connected in their common experiences of movement and marginality, they may tap into their Christian identity to claim belonging to the Bay and other social groups. Thus migrant members of the Bay are not necessarily displaced and isolated in Cape Town but invest in diverse social relationships and sources of capital. This negotiation of social boundaries makes migrants 'frontier people' (Kopytoff 1987). While many of the migrants in this book have formed close relationships with other migrants, their membership at a mixed denominational church challenges this notion of distance. When Lisa first came to Cape Town she joined the same church that she belonged to in Zimbabwe –Christ Embassy. I interviewed Lisa about her decision to join the Bay:

'I was at Christ Embassy at home and I thought I would find belonging there. I thought I should because the Zimbabweans I know here, many of them also go to Christ Embassy. But actually I felt at home with the style but not the people... Some people might

45

avoid me in church or not respond to my greeting, but mostly at the Bay everyone is friendly... At the Bay we meet many different people which I like... It's true my closest friends are other Zimbabweans and not necessarily people who go to the Bay but I chose not to go to a 'Zimbabwean' church because the people there know each other and each other's business too well. They like to gossip and talk about each other. They say how did she afford that? How did she manage to get that job? At the Bay there isn't gossip like that." [25]

Lisa joined Christ Embassy because of familiarity and to tap into potential networks with other Zimbabweans in Cape Town. However, the familiarity also had negative consequences in terms of the relationships she formed. By tapping into her habitus as a Zimbabwean, Lisa was able to form friendships with people who speak the same language and have a similar socio-cultural reference. By tapping into her habitus as a Christian, on the other hand, Lisa has also been able to negotiate networks and intimacy and distance in those networks. Her choice of belonging to a church with a diverse congregation highlights Owen's (2011: 114) contention that networks that span race, class, gender, and ethnicity are highly important for migrants' survival. For the Congolese migrants in her study, forming networks is a "way of life" at home and abroad. In their host communities, however, social and economic capital are more difficult for migrants to attain and requires a more active and strategic pursuit of social connections with as many of the "right others" as possible.

---

[25] Interview with Lisa at her home in Capricorn (28 July 2012).

Transmigrants, Gielis (2009: 601) argues, experience symbolic and mental borders which can act as barriers to new worlds but also create openings. Transmigrants are able to tap into a "transnational habitus" (Gielis 2009: 603) which they can draw on to survive in a new country, but they also reinforce other borders on a personal level in order to maintain a sense of being part of their former world, despite physical distance. This 'border experience' means that migrants can claim intimacy as well as distance when needed. As my conversation with Lisa highlighted, this has implications for the ways in which conviviality is experienced at the Bay.

Gregory joined the Bay in order to navigate personal ties in the church. On August 3rd, 2012, I sat with Gregory at his home in Capricorn. I asked him why he joined the Bay and whether he had visited other churches or just the Bay since arriving in Cape Town. His response elicited some important insights into the ways in which migrants negotiate their agency and networks inter-subjectively:

"[I have] Just [been to] the Bay. My uncle brought me here. I always followed his religion because I lived with him. Well I always followed the family I stayed with, that's why my religion is different to my brother and mother for example."

Gregory joined the Bay because that was where his uncle attended and having lived with his uncle as a child and adolescent it seemed inevitable for him to attend the same church in his in his new home, Cape Town. It would seem that Gregory's individual choice in the matter was limited. His uncle was his sole connection in Cape Town and his initial provider. As Levitt and Glick Schiller (2004) contend, the transnational social field is partly composed of family ties. Yet Gregory decided to be baptised, to make the Bay his religious home and since his uncle left in early 2012 Gregory has become a Home Group leader. Gregory described his experience with baptism:

> *"[At the Bay] they say you aren't born a Christian you become one. [laughs] I never heard it like that. As a child you just follow with your parents. So I was encouraged to be baptised like that. It took some time. Actually I was only baptised recently... Being baptised, oh Paula, that was amazing. You know when they pour that cold water on you, you are wet and cold but you know that now Jesus is with you for real. And now the Bay is my church... Being baptised means I belong. You can't really belong if you haven't been baptised in the Holy Spirit."*[26]

Gregory's decision to join the Bay and to be baptised, not unlike his decision to come to Cape Town, was neither a purely individual, nor a purely imposed one. Agency is often emphasised as being an individual navigation of social structure, but Nyamnjoh (2002) argues that it also concerns how individuals navigate their agency inter-subjectively, negotiating collective interests and seeking conviviality and belonging.

My interview with Gregory highlighted that while social ties come into play in the decision to join a church, the decision is not necessarily a conscious attempt to gain social capital. Owen (2011: 187; 195) highlights that migrants select churches for a variety of reasons, and not solely out of a rational interest in another's prospective social resources (nor are they necessarily even aware of the capital another person

---

[26] Interview with Gregory at his home in Capricorn (3 August 2012).

or an organisation might have). More embodied notions of faith are also part of the choice to join a church (Mahler and Hansing 2005). Spiritual or religious capital is useful for understanding the combination of esoteric, personal and social forces that inform a person's decision to join a church. Verter (2003: 158) defines spiritual capital as a cultural resource to be acquired, exchanged and used to mobilise resources. In line with Bourdieu, Verter (2003: 158) argues that the acquisition of this capital is further acquired in the context of existing power structures.

Religious capital is the "degree of mastery of and attachment to a particular religious culture" (Stark and Finke 2000: 120; Iannaconne 1990). According to Finke (2003: 3), emotional attachment to a religion is a component of religious capital, and "religious experiences often form an emotional bond that greatly enhances the productive capacity of religious capital." Comaroff and Comaroff (2009) contend that ethnicity is drawn on for a variety of motives such as gaining access to land and legal rights, but the terms of its existence must also be proven and performed and may entail strong emotional ties. Similarly, while Christian identity may be drawn on in order to access a variety of capitals, it is also rooted in very real, esoteric and emotional experiences and built and performed via ritual and worship. Thus belonging may be at once spiritual, emotional, strategic and inter-subjective.

Drawing on Christian Habitus and Spiritual Capital at the Bay

Joseph joined the Bay because of what he termed *"a shared love of Jesus."*[27] He described the importance of being a Christian both in terms of his spirituality and intimate knowledge of God as well as his identity, which allowed him to be at home anywhere "where there is a move of the spirit." He explained:

> *"Paula I am home anywhere that Jesus speaks to me. We are all at home and one in Christ. If someone is not nice to me here because I am from Malawi or maybe another reason, I say ok, because I know Jesus is with me...I have my Christian identity first... People at the Bay mostly know Jesus so I can relate to them...In Christ you are always home Paula."*[28]

Although Joseph was 'at home' in the Bay due to its particular form of worship and habitus, he also drew on his Christian identity in order to navigate other forms of worship at unfamiliar churches and create networks outside of the Bay. He elaborated, "I like to see how other places worship; it is refreshing. God loves us all even if we do things differently. I am Christian wherever I go... It is good to meet other Christians because God wants us to be one Kingdom." When I have asked Joseph about Malawi the conversation quickly steered towards his *"home in God."* Joseph's deep devotion to Christ gave him a sense of strength and stability in the context of the uncertainty of migration and he was among few migrants at the Bay considered a leader.

---

[27] Interview with Joseph at his home in Capricorn (11 August 2012).
[28] Interview with Joseph at his home in Capricorn (23 August 2012).

Habitus, as defined by Bourdieu (1990: 53) is a set of dispositions instilled through time spent in, and perhaps adapting to a particular social field. Habitus can be considered second nature and may reproduce existing structures. Via individual agency, people may generate new behaviours and responses; however these remain within the "constraints and limits initially set on its interventions" (Bourdieu 1990: 55). This is evident when people adapt to new social fields, but also in how they may consciously recognise and emphasise a shared habitus in forming relationships. While there are aspects of Joseph's habitus that allowed him to feel at home at the Bay, he also conveyed a different set of norms. Andre, a devoted member of the Bay described the ways in which he and Joseph had to negotiate common terms for their relationship.

"I think Joseph came from a more hierarchical church background. Leaders really take on a guidance role in your life. And I think Joseph wanted that from me. He would send me text messages asking for advice and sometimes even more material things like money or rides to places. It was getting too close and I felt like he wanted a father or a brother. That's not me. I really had to explain to him that I didn't see myself as a leader. God is the only true leader. Now he sends me text messages offering me guidance and prayers and he calls to check on me sometimes. It is more brotherly now and we do actually support each other a lot... I also ask him to pray for me sometimes." [29]

Joseph's approach to leadership is in line with Englund's (2003) description of the way in which Pentecostals in Malawi subscribe their subjectivity to a higher power, seeking to be

[29] Interview with Andre in Muizenberg (21 August 2012)

enlightened from those individuals who appear especially spiritually gifted or well networked. Hierarchy is actively embraced and seen as necessary for enlightenment. Andre was seen as someone in a position of hierarchy to provide structured spiritual guidance. However, for Andre conviviality was maintained through the negotiation of these expectations, requiring an adaptation on both Joseph and Andre's part. In some cases being able to draw on relationships for material support is not welcomed, as in the case of Joseph and Andre, but relationships can also be drawn on for non-material support. In the following section I will discuss the ways in which conviviality at the Bay is tied to the ways in which the church provides bonding and bridging forms of capital.

Bridging and Bonding Capital

Putnam (2000) emphasises social capital as a 'connective tissue' which holds society together and is a social good in an age of increasing individualism. Social relationships are a source of trust and reciprocity, much like civic obligations and virtue and are "most powerful when embedded in a dense network of reciprocal social relations" (Putnam 2000: 19). Bonding social capital is the building of connections between members of a group and serves to strengthen social cohesion. Bridging social capital on the other hand links members of different social groups, resulting in wider networks (Putnam 2000: 22).

Bridging Capital

The Bay provides members opportunities to participate in the institutional aspects of the church by offering courses for those who wish to become Home Group leaders. The church initiated Fire Starters, a course for Home Group participants to deepen their understanding of worship and the bible. The course was held every Wednesday evening for eight weeks and created a space of sociality and collective worship where members that might otherwise not interact could spend time face to face with people of diverse backgrounds (see Ammerman and Farnsley 1997: 57). Bridging capital can be drawn on for formal and informal support during difficult times and enhance feelings of social solidarity (Foley *et al.* 2001: 220).

At the Bay this capital has also become transnational. The Bay is tied to the Bay Democratic Republic of Congo (DRC), a church formed in 2011 by Antoine and Mattie, a couple from the DRC that had attended the Bay while living in South Africa. The connection between the Bay and the Bay DRC is at the level of individuals and lay leaders, as the Bay DRC is not linked to large scale international umbrella organisations such as New Frontiers. Although the Bay does not provide direct support (financial or administrative), support comes in other, more symbolic forms. For example, the Bay supported Mattie and Antoine in organising a funeral for the child they lost in 2011 and with celebrating a baby shower in 2012. Mattie described the relationship with the Bay as a friendship because "they don't give us money... We just like to see them. They give us spiritual support. And also when I come here I am motivated again to work at home [DRC]."[30] In his work on Pentecostalism in Malawi, Englund (2003) explores the 'planting' of churches by local religious leaders in order to claim independency from large foreign churches. These 'independent' churches prefer to draw on their networks for a variety of support and negotiate their

---

[30] Interview with Mattie at the Bay Community Church (21 October 2012).

independency rather than being passive recipients of hand outs from more advantaged churches in other parts of the world. Mattie and Antoine did not plant the Bay DRC in order claim independence from a perceived enslavement to wealthier churches and they have not pursued financial support from the Bay. However, their pursuit of other interests such as spiritual support and a 'home away from home' in Cape Town are alternative ways of connecting beyond financial support through a two-way negotiation of relationships.

Relationships formed at the Bay also create other forms of capital. Several of the migrants I worked with such as Gregory and Lisa have received employment opportunities by getting to know South African members of the church, and in some cases other more established migrant members. This may require negotiating with the intimacy of personal relations, which is something that I experienced personally. Over the Christmas 2012/2013 period I received a call from Joseph asking if I could send Miriam money as she was struggling to get home from Mpumalanga. Although I had offered Miriam assistance with other matters, I did not feel in a position to send the amount of money she needed. Yet I grappled with feeling obligated and had to consider which course of action would still allow us to remain friends without hard feelings.

Bridging capital may also have to be negotiated on the basis of criteria for inclusion or exclusion. At the Bay, religious identity is the primary basis for inclusion. However, there are other aspects of inclusion and exclusion that also come to the fore in church interactions. I attended a youth group meeting in July 2012.[31] Youth aged 14-18 from around

[31] Held on 13 July 2012.

Muizenberg, Capricorn and nearby suburbs flooded into the church hall. Waiting for the youth service to start, I chatted with Julian, a leader of the youth group at the church and studying politics at the University of Cape Town. Some of the youth were playing rambunctiously and Julian remarked:

> *"You see, we are all equal in the church and even though these people were not educated in the same way as you and I, like about manners and things, they come from a different context and that is ok here. We are all supposed to be one Kingdom even with differences."*

Julian's commitment to church work, while patronising, is not exclusive. Religion at the Bay is ultimately a greater criterion for inclusion than other differences. Furthermore, a righteous commitment to the 'one Kingdom' ideology provides a framework with which to include those that might be considered radically different in other contexts.

Sheldon described the Bay's emphasis on being open and inclusive but also highlighted that the church has had to enforce certain requirements for inclusion:

> *"The church is divided and broken into all these different styles... The Kingdom is actually all mixed. The bible speaks about we are one. Location has been a big one but this [place] is a true expression of what it should look like... We have had to deal with some things. Like people that come for food packages on Saturdays have to be part of a Home Group. It's not like we are forcing anyone to do anything, it's just that it is part of having a relationship with the church, rather than us just giving hand-outs."*[32]

---

[32] On 19 July, 2012.

Sheldon did not seem surprised that people would join the church solely for hand outs but the church negotiated the varying notions of what should be provided by putting in place practical conditions for inclusion. This also enables the 'one Kingdom' ideology to be enacted. By requiring people that might otherwise come to church just for food to join a Home Group, the church is able to further fulfil its spiritual mission to spread the word of God and save souls, along with the mission to serve the poor. Gregory, Joseph and Miriam all received food packages on Saturday and are also required to volunteer periodically to package and deliver food. When I enquired with them about receiving food, Miriam did not seem to want to discuss the matter, perhaps feeling that it reflected poorly on the independence she was striving for. [33] Joseph was quick to emphasise that God provides through the church and the volunteerism is required because everyone must give something of themselves to the church. He also stressed the 'one Kingdom' identity of the church –noting that "we are all one so if some members of the church are poor, we have to get together to help them. And we all have something to give. We are all part of God's plan." The church's 'one Kingdom' identity enabled the church and its members to negotiate criteria for inclusion and in Joseph's case, aspects of his life such as poverty which might otherwise make him feel excluded.

Bonding Capital

While the facilitation of mutually supportive relationships between Bay members contributes to its 'one Kingdom' identity, this must be negotiated and is not always achieved.

---

[33] When spending time with Miriam and Joseph in Capricorn (16 September 2012).

Members may still have differential access to that capital, especially in terms of church leadership. One member shared that he felt that those with a certain level of education and standing in their professional lives, a certain 'habitus', are still more likely to have access to higher level positions. The "*white middle class identity is still pretty obvious and I see it in the leadership decisions that the church makes.*"[34] As businesses were closing for the Christmas 2012/ 2013 holidays, the Bay also held closing events, one of which was a braai for all members as well as separate braais for Home Groups from different areas, the 'Capricorn group' being one of them. I sat with Gregory, Joseph and a few members of their recently started Home Group. They were planning their modest meal for the Capricorn group braai. I asked if they would attend the big braai with all the members. Joseph responded that they were not able to pay for so much food so preferred to go only to the Capricorn group braai where people would bring similar items and might be more likely to share. This event served to inadvertently create a divide between migrants and other members.

Although there are moments when divisions were amplified, the Bay was predominantly described to me as a 'home' and a "safe place,"[35] a space in which it may be possible to negotiate fears of the 'other'. Gregory described his elation at eating with white people during an Africa Evening hosted by the Bay in February 2011. Migrant members cooked traditional dishes for the event and tickets were sold to approximately 100 Bay members. Lindi, the leader of Prayer Furnace and organiser of the event expressed

---

[34] Discussion at after church service at the Bay Community Church (16 September 2012).
[35] Interview with Miriam at her home in Capricorn (7 August 2012).

disappointment that more members of the church did not feel it was important enough to attend. However, Gregory's experience was different:

> "I had never eaten with white people and I never thought I would get that chance. It was amazing to sit at the table together like that. I thought wow, this is it in South Africa... I thought white people would eat so differently but they didn't."[36]

Miriam is one of the few locals at the Bay and has confessed to me that she was afraid to join the Bay because it was a 'white church' (a fear she believed is one of the reasons many black South Africans have not joined the Bay). She explained to me why she joined the Bay:

> "This woman from Lavender Hill gave me a flier and encouraged me to go. I was very curious because it is such a big church and I had heard of it before... I went one Sunday and even though I was nervous –I didn't think my English was good enough and I was not used to conversing with white people. But after the first time I felt I should go again... The next time I went this woman came to the bathroom to prophesize to me. She told me Miriam you should not be afraid, God has many plans for you. I couldn't believe it. After that I felt so differently Paula. I was not afraid. Everything at the Bay has helped me to be less fearful. I can talk to anyone now and I feel equal." [37]

Sichone (2008) suggests that the true cosmopolitan might be the local person who experiences the world through relationships with foreigners, even if he or she has never

---

[36] Interview with Gregory at his home in Capricorn (9 July 2012).
[37] Interview with Miriam at her home in Capricorn (7 August 2012).

physically left home. In Sichone's (2008) sense of the word, Miriam is a cosmopolitan. Miriam frequently asked me about home, emphasizing her love of travel and novelty. I asked her if she feels like an outsider in Cape Town. She responded:

> *"Yes in some ways. I am Zulu and most of the people here are Xhosa so they also know I am not from here. But also I like to meet new people and sometimes I find something in common with them that can make us good friends."*[38]

Miriam's experience signifies that being foreign could more broadly mean being an outsider, whether South African or not. It also signifies that being an outsider or insider is negotiated through relationships and attitude towards so-called foreigners and locals. Miriam and Joseph, who have a close bond, share a love of exploring different forms of worship and are both involved in Prayer Furnace and leading a Home Group. Sichone (2003: 138) presents case studies of women who take a preference for foreign men, contending that there are times when people "stick together because they are alike and there are times when people stick together because they are different." Miriam negotiated her status as a foreigner and insider by befriending a wide range of people, facilitated by the Bay and her Christian identity.

Nyamnjoh (2007b: 2) contends that even in the context of transnational belonging and relationships with locals, it is difficult to really feel "at home away from home" given the fixation with authenticity and bounded notions of home. That being said, bounded notions of home ignore the relationships that have formed between locals and foreigners, citizens and subjects and Nyamnjoh (2007b: 2) argues in

---

[38] Discussion with Miriam during a driving lesson (12 August 2012).

favour of greater attention being paid to examples of "flexible, negotiated, cosmopolitan and popular forms of citizenship." Hannerz (1989 in Glick Schiller *et al.* 2006: 10) similarly emphasises the tendency of people to engage in processes of "creolization", creative interpretation of cultural flows that counteracts notions of homogenisation. Thus while Miriam is on the one hand a victim of diminishing circles of belonging, feeling like an outsider in her own country, she is also an active participant in increasing circles of belonging (see Nyamnjoh 2007a), facilitated by the Bay and initiated by her own independent spirit, curiosity, and warmth. She is an example of Schopenhaur's description of the porcupine with "a great deal of internal warmth" who "preferred to stay apart from the group, and so caused and encountered the least trouble" (Luepnitz 2002: 249).

Conclusion

In this chapter I investigated the Bay Community Church as convivial space and a 'home away from home' for its migrant members. I explored the ways in which migrants are able to draw on different habituses in order to exist in many worlds at once and to maintain convivial relationships. Conviviality was conceptualised as a constant process of building and remaking relationships in order to achieve a balance between getting close but not too close.

I have argued that conviviality is facilitated by the Charismatic style of worship which encourages free movement, spontaneity and intimate physical interaction such as hugging. Drawing on Warnier's (2006; 2009) work on the technologies of material culture I explored the ways in which worshippers come to identify themselves as vessels for God's love and grace. Conviviality becomes inscribed on the body and is expressed in physical intimacy between worshippers who do not necessarily know each other outside of services. Through rituals, church activities and the 'one Kingdom' identity of the Bay, the church provides bridging and bonding capital which connects members from different social groups and widens networks, as well as strengthens these relationships. The emphasis on being one Kingdom encourages a reconciliation of tensions towards convivial relations and religion ultimately becomes a greater criterion for inclusion than other differences.

Outside of worship, the church is the site of transnational and local networks which migrants draw on for social and spiritual capital, emphasizing a shared Christian identity and habitus. Many migrants at the Bay are linked to international and local Pentecostal organisations in Cape Town and in their home countries, establishing multifarious translational linkages that go beyond the common global-local dichotomy. Networks and relationships are important for migrants, often considered outsider 'others' and looked upon negatively by 'locals' in Cape Town. Membership with a mixed denominational church challenges the notion that migrants stick to themselves. Although conviviality is not a constant state of relations at the Bay, it is largely considered a 'home away from home' for migrants and a space in which it is possible to safely negotiate fears or misconceptions about the 'other', whether migrant or local.

In the chapter that follows I demonstrate the ways in which migrants use ICTs to negotiate relationships at the Bay and to acquire social and spiritual capital.

Chapter 4

Inside And Outside, Intimacy and Distance: Migrants' Use Of Information and Communication Technologies in the Context of the Bay Community Church

Introduction

In Chapter Three, I argued that conviviality at the Bay Community Church is not a constant state of relations but a process of building and remaking relationships in order to achieve a balance between intimacy and distance. Conviviality is inscribed on the body through free and spontaneous worship and enables intimate interactions with people who do not necessarily engage with one another outside of church. The church further provides bridging and bonding capital which widens the social networks of its members. Migrants draw on their Christian habitus to find belonging at the church and they are able to forge relationships that allow them to belong in many places at once. This can require a negotiation of the obligations that belonging to many networks may imply such as family responsibilities, personal desires and spiritual beliefs. It also requires reconciling conflicting expectations, as actors in networks may have a variety of interests and aspirations.

In this chapter I argue that ICTs, particularly the cell phone, are implicated in migrants' formation of networks, acquisition of social and spiritual capital, and formation of convivial relationships. Drawing on de Bruijn *et al.*'s (2009) argument that technology shapes the user just as the user shapes the technology, I investigate how these technologies shape users' bodies, and how the users in turn shape the technologies (e.g. through ring tones and mannerisms).

While technologies allow for the transcendence of certain boundaries they may also impose new boundaries through their use. Ties to home are important in the emotional lives of migrants but the boundaries of physical distance and familial obligations can also be stretched with opportunism, facilitated by mobile communication technology (Nyamnjoh 2005). This must be negotiated by individuals inter-subjectively. Similarly, migrants may pursue wealthier members of their church with demands for material assistance justified by notions of the church as a family and members as brothers and sisters in Christ.

ICTs are implicated in the ways in which migrants construct their identity in order to belong. In particular, migrants use Facebook and text messaging to emphasise their Christian identity. Facebook is also used by migrants to construct a 'successful' identity for themselves, often based on a false picture of life in South Africa. This picture of success can serve to further intensify financial and social obligations for migrants which are difficult to manage.

Reaching the Kingdom

Worship and church events can be important for integration because they reinforce the religious identity of migrants which is the common basis for belonging in the church and possibly their host countries as well (Goliama 2010: 160). At the Bay, connectivity to church life is facilitated by the phone. Through their cell phones migrants can be kept up to date with church events. The Bay uses a program called MyMessager to send text messages out to all members. Not all members have email or regular access to email, Sheldon explained to me, but almost everyone has a cell phone. [39] Being able to know what is happening at the church enables migrants to negotiate belonging and facilitates bridging capital. Miriam joined Prayer Furnace because she received text messages about weekly meetings and eventually decided to attend. Although the messages were essentially mass information notices, she described them as invitations, almost as though they were meant for her alone. The interpretation of these messages as invitations encouraged Miriam to feel included and attend, despite feeling strange initially about being the only black person in the group. [40]

Cell phones were used among the 'Capricorn Group' to coordinate around church events such as getting to and from Fire Starters since few in this group had a car. Before the first three Home Group meetings I attended, Gregory and Diana each sent me two text messages a week to remind me that Home Group meetings were taking place. The messages were a practical reminder, especially when there was a location change, and also made me feel welcome.

As I discussed in Chapter Three, the church braai events at Christmas time inadvertently created a divide between the 'Capricorn group', largely migrants, and other church members, as the group felt they could not afford to attend both events. Joseph and Diana were able to coordinate the Capricorn group using cell phones so that the group as a whole could make a decision to attend both or just one event. Diana and Joseph sent text messages to all of the group members and Joseph led a meeting. With cell phones, the

[39] On 19 July 2012.
[40] Interview with Miriam at her home in Capricorn (7 August 2012).

Capricorn group could coordinate and negotiate being outsiders as a group.

The church uses MyMessager to send text messages to a group of individuals who are involved in prayer networks. They are notified that someone needs a prayer and are asked to take time to speak with God about this particular person. Sheldon emphasised that God always hears people. In other words, one does not need a cell phone to get in touch with God. However, he indicated that cell phones are very practical for doing God's work, allowing for a quick mobilisation of prayer forces and organizing large scale prayer events. [41]

ICTs also facilitate bonding between members. Joseph informed me that he and Miriam send each other text messages if they need a prayer for something specific. He showed me one such text message from Miriam asking him: "Joseph please pray that God shows me the way to a job." [42] Requesting a prayer has several implications for the formation and maintenance of relationships between members. In asking him to pray for her, Miriam revealed intimate desires to Joseph, establishing trust. Although it would be hard to measure the effects of the prayer itself, Joseph has also asked Miriam for prayers, reciprocating with intimate details. In Chapter Three, I discussed the relationship between Andre and Joseph, members of the church from different socio-economic classes and countries, who negotiated the roles in their relationship. For Andre, the shift from a more 'father-son' relationship to a more desired brotherly one was represented by a decline in requests for leadership, advice and

---

[41] On 19 July 2012.
[42] While spending time with Miriam and Joseph (2 December 2012).

material goods from Joseph. A common basis was found in being able to pray for each other.

As Andre told me:

> "...Now he [Joseph] sends me text messages offering me guidance and prayers and he calls to check on me sometimes. It is more brotherly now and we do actually support each other a lot... I also ask him to pray for me sometimes".[43]

No matter one's financial or social status, all members of the church can pray and almost all church members can send and receive text message requests for prayers.

Gregory sent me one request for a prayer: "GOD is faithful I will make it, please keep praying for me" in reference to arranging for his girlfriend to travel from Malawi to Cape Town.[44] However, I mostly received text messages from church members to let me know that they were praying for me or that God was with me. Since church members were aware that I was not Christian, it became important for them to send me messages conveying the power of God and praying for me. I received a text message from Miriam saying, "Paula, oh Paula, we thank God for bringing you into our lives and pray that he will lead you in his plan,"[45] and a text message from Gregory stating "GOD bless you Paula. I know that God is watching over you."[46] These messages highlighted the potential for the phone to be a tool of conversion and sociality in God. The cell phone allows for limited and targeted mass communication and the sender

---

[43] Interview with Andre in Muizenberg (21 August 2012).
[44] Text message received from Gregory (15 January 2013).
[45] Text message received from Miriam (7 August 2012).
[46] Text message received from Gregory (8 September 2012).

cannot be denied contact in the sense that they can be ignored before the message has been delivered, as may be the case with more traditional methods of spreading God's word (e.g. going door to door, handing out fliers).

I enquired with Joseph about the significance of sending a text message prayer request as opposed to a telephone call. His response both referred to the economic benefits of text messages and the practical implications of sending a text over a phone call: "It is better to send a text message because it is shorter the person can pray whenever they feel God moving through them."[47] The request can be fulfilled at a moment that is convenient to the receiver, while a phone call might require a more immediate response. The request for a prayer coming in the form of a text message serves to mediate the intimacy of requesting a prayer, and can also allow for wider networking. Joseph told me that when he has a problem, he requests a wide range of people to pray for him as he can send the same text message to many people at once.

Brothers and Sisters in Christ

Palmer *et al.* (2009: 122) explore kinship in religion, highlighting that most religions use family kinship terms such as father, mother, brother, sister and child to describe fellow members. This broadly includes parent-child-like relationships between religious leaders and their followers and sibling-like relationships among co-followers. In the religious context, communicating acceptance of supernatural claims is aimed at influencing the behaviour of others usually transmitted from ancestors to descendants across generations. Palmer *et al.* (2009:110) argue that religious

---

[47] Spending time with Miriam and Joseph (2 December 2012).

traditions were perpetuated because they "increased cooperation among co-descendants by communicating the willingness to accept the influence of each other and their common ancestors." They conclude that religious behaviour and the incorporation of followers into kinship-like relations promote cooperative social relationships.

In Christianity, the extension of kinship to fellow worshippers is reflected in the bible when Paul calls his co-Christians "brothers and sisters" in letters to the apostle (Aasgaard 2004: 2). When I asked Joseph about belonging to a church with such a diverse congregation, his response that "we are brothers and sisters in Christ"[48] reflected the alternative or complementary kinship that Christianity provides. Levine (2008: 376) highlights that kinship in developed, globalising contexts is instituted over time through practises and processes. This contrasts with notions of kinship as being fixed, as classic kinship studies, largely conducted in non-western pre-industrial 'kinship-based' societies, suggested (Levine 2008: 377). Gregory's description of his upbringing in Malawi reflected the encompassing nature of extended families and kinship. Gregory and his biological brothers and sisters were spread amongst extended family; uncles and aunts filled in as fathers and mothers, cousins became siblings and younger cousins became nieces and nephews. Migration has further undone the prototypical family (Miller 2010) and there exists an assortment of alternative and complementary family forms. Levine (2008: 383) claims that people may create meaningful networks based on alternative notions of kin in the context of exclusion. Instances of alternative kin, Levine (2008: 378) argues, illustrate that "individuals can manipulate the range of

---

[48] Spending time with Joseph (2 December 2012)

options of available to them to secure personally desirable marital and family arrangements". Levitt and Glick Schiller (2004: 19) emphasise that migrants "actively pursue or neglect blood ties and fictitious kinship" based on their individual needs.

Weston (1995: 108-113) describes alternative kinship relationships as a fluid network of individuals who can be replaced as circumstances or personal preferences change. This is exemplified among migrants in their appropriation of fellow worshippers as kin in order to maintain convivial relationships. Alternative kinship in the church can fulfil similar or different functions to other kinship relations. Pentecostal churches emphasise breaking from the past, represented by ties to family and traditions (Meyer 1998). Although the Bay does not preach breaking from family ties, conversion may precipitate this. For the Bay as an institution, breaking with the past involves detaching from legalistic religious doctrine and movements that do not recognise 'gifts of the spirit' (e.g. spontaneous healing, speaking in tongues). For the individual this might entail disconnecting from activities and relationships not occurring in the spirit of God, which in some cases may demand a break from kin. In Miriam's case, being a Christian distanced her from family traditions, and pushed her to enter new social and personal relationships such as with Joseph. Like Miriam, Lisa and Joseph live far away from home and also sought kin-like relationships outside of their families due to their desire for independence and familial obligations that can make kinship ties more burdensome than supportive. They have not done away with biological kin but have added a different, more supportive set of kin to their repertoire.

70

Having 'brothers and sisters' in Christ can extend the notion of who can be called upon for support. ICTs are also implicated in the negotiation of extended kinship ties. When Miriam struggled to get back to Cape Town from Mpumalanga after the Christmas holidays she did not call upon family but on several church members for assistance. She sent text messages to three close friends with whom she socialised outside of church and Joseph made phone calls to six people with whom Miriam interacted with only in the church context, predominantly white middle class members. I asked her why she called upon these particular people and whether she received help. Miriam replied:

> "I trusted those people to come through for me because they are fellow Christians and members of the Bay. People at the Bay are supportive of each other because we all belong there and love each other as Christians… I only asked the people that I trusted… Not everyone has the means even if they wanted to help. And they were not all able to assist me… Some of them I felt I would not ask them again… It made the struggle harder but that is ok… I trust God's plan."

I also enquired about Joseph's role in requesting assistance on Miriam's behalf. Miriam responded:

> "I wanted to call people because it is more polite than sending a text and Joseph offered to help because of the airtime costs… He is good with people and knows everyone at the Bay. He has their numbers so he could contact them even if they were away for the holidays…I didn't want to seem like begging."[49]

---

[49] Interview with Miriam at her home in Capricorn (12 January 2013).

Miriam emphasised that Joseph called because of the airtime costs but she also conceded that she did not want to appear to be begging. I could hear the disappointment in Miriam's voice when she described being turned down and later Joseph informed me that he had called in part to ease the disappointment of a negative answer. [50] Using a cell phone to appeal to people for assistance on her behalf, as a brother would help a sister, he was also able to reduce her feeling of begging. Although Miriam may have felt that the church provided the basis for more kin-like relations between members, she also had to negotiate the discomfort of requesting money. The cell phone was useful in this regard because Joseph was able to make phone calls from afar (seemingly more polite than text messages) while still maintaining a more comfortable distance than asking in person. Several church members assisted Miriam, perhaps out of a sense of kinship and Christian duty, and she was able to return to Cape Town. Other members did not assist Miriam and she mentioned that she would reconsider who she could rely on.

Inside and Outside: the Cell Phone and the Body

The cell phone is used by migrants to maintain contact with home but the obstacles related to connectivity and physical boundaries mean that distance cannot be entirely overcome. This reflects Goggin's (2012: 102) argument that cell phone technology is tied into power relations of consumption. The cell phone must also be understood in the context of globalisation as a process of cultural flows that intersect in complex and disjunctured ways (Appadurai 2000).

---

[50] Interview with Joseph at his home in Capricorn (25 January 2013).

For example, Lisa's contact with home (highlighted in the fieldwork excerpt 'Lisa and her Cell Phones' in the text box on the following page) is limited by cost and distance, all tied into her position in Cape Town as a migrant from Zimbabwe, forced by economic conditions to leave home.

Lisa and her Cell Phones[51]

Lisa and I were having lunch at her home in Capricorn when her phone rang and then stopped. Her body tensed as the phone suddenly rang and she grabbed it anxiously to see who was calling. She asked if I would mind if she made a call. Picking up another phone, Lisa began typing in the number from the phone that had been called. She stood up impatiently as she waited for the phone to ring and paced the room. She immediately entered into a serious conversation, raising her voice and repeating her words slowly, looking at the phone to see if it was still connected. As I was unable to understand the content of the conversation in Shona, I focused on her facial expressions and hand gestures. Although the person on the other end could not see her, Lisa's animated hand gestures suggested she was speaking to someone in front of her. As she listened attentively to the voice on the other end, her facial expressions loosened and she smiled. When she hung up, I asked if she would mind telling me about the conversation.

L: That was my sister. She is looking after my son and he was ill a few days ago.

P: You seemed annoyed when you first picked up the phone.

L: The connection is sometimes bad and I was so worried about him and then I couldn't hear what she said. But she says he

---

[51] Interview with Lisa at her home in Capricorn (28 July 2012).

is getting better. I spoke to him very briefly but he is so shy with me on the phone.

P: Is it expensive to call home?

L: [rolls her eyes and shakes her head] Yes it is so expensive, but it is cheaper for me than for them.

P: Why do you have two cell phones?

L: Well I had the first one and some business contacts in Cape Town have that number and my family also uses that number but my other phone has a different SIM which is cheaper to call home so I keep both.

My conversation with Lisa led me to consider the enabling and limiting aspects of cell phone use. While Lisa was able to get news of her son from across the border, she struggled to connect immediately and her physical reactions to the conversation reflected the frustration and angst experienced when trying to communicate with faulty technology or via poor networks. I could hear Lisa's despair as she said that her son was shy with her on the phone. We spoke later about her son being far away. While Lisa emphasised the material aspects of his life that were better, such as more affordable education, safety, and maintaining contact with cousins who would be like brothers and sisters to him in the future, her husband interrupted her and spoke frankly: "she misses him a lot but it is basically better education." Miller (2010) describes the use of the cell phone by migrant Philippine and Caribbean families in order to keep in touch with their children. He highlights that while the cell phone connects children and parents, particularly children and mothers, rather than easing the distance this contact reinforces an idealised relationship, leading to intense feelings of abandonment and disappointment (Miller 2010: 123).

Lisa's use of two cell phones was interesting. Campbell (2005a: 25) highlights that many people using the Internet make little distinction between life online and life offline. Being online is part of everyday social existence and maintaining relationships and networks online is just as important as maintaining relationships offline. For Lisa, having two cell phones reflects the importance of being reached and reaching out. She does not want to discard of a cell phone because she may lose out on possible business. Lisa emphasised her education to me and distinguished herself from other domestic workers who will "take anything they are given... I don't take my employers' old clothes and food and medicine. If they want to give me something, they should give it to me. I don't need hand outs."[52] Thus her 'business' cell phone is part of her wider identity construction as a business woman – not a servant. During my conversation with her, I observed Lisa checking both phones periodically – doubling her chances of communication.

Lisa's bodily reactions while communicating on the phone reflected the implications for the body in negotiating physical and social boundaries. According to Warnier (2006), the human body uses technologies to negotiate physical and social boundaries of the external world to extend beyond its own physical limitations. The body is a container of thoughts and emotions which can be communicated with material technologies such as ICTs. The nation state, as a container of bodies, provides an opening through its borders but applies strict control over what or who is considered an "insider" or "outsider" (Warnier 2006: 191). Bodies are effectively connected across these borders by sensori-motor engagement with keyboards, cell phone speakers, webcams, etc. with

---

[52] On 28 July 2012.

which the acting subject engages cognitively and emotionally. Just as the perception of a blind person is felt at the end of his or her walking stick as opposed to between the stick and the surface of his or her hand, ICTs can become extensions of a person's own communication tools such as voice, hearing, and sight. Warnier (2006: 193) further emphasises that transformations takes place in passing through a border from one container to another. The body reacts and responds to the technology by undertaking certain physical and emotional adjustments. The act of using ICTs requires adjustment of the body, in order to represent oneself to another person and to overcome the limitations of technology (sound quality, cost) such as speaking louder or only giving basic information. It may also require an emotional acceptance of the limits of long distance relationships.

In Chapter Three I highlighted that ritual techniques of the body lead worshippers to identify themselves as vessels containing God or through which God works. Many of the migrants I spent time with communicated spiritual texts, prayers, and words of encouragement via text message or Facebook. These may affect a bodily reaction for the person on the other end – they may feel the presence of God or feel motivated to pray (see Warnier 2006). The cell phone in that sense is a medium for accessing the Holy Spirit. Gregory described the importance of receiving spiritual messages from home, usually as a Facebook message:

> *'When I get prayers from home it means that person is thinking of me but also that God is thinking of me and is working*

through that person. Especially like when my cousin sends me a prophecy. That is God working through them.[53]

The physical adjustments associated with cell phones further reflects the notion put forth by Latour (2005) and Callon (1991) that agency is not solely exercised by human actors. According to Actor Network Theory (ANT) (Latour 2005 and Callon 1991), both humans and non-human items such as cell phones are considered agents (termed 'actants') in a network. Although only human actors can put actants into circulation in the network, non-human agents can exercise influence on human actors; actants and actors are created in interaction with each other (Goggin 2012: 11). Neither technology nor society should be taken as a given; cell phones and their use by actors, in that sense, are a "work in progress" (Goggin 2012: 12).

Calling on God

Campbell (2005b) contends that cell phones are governed by the hierarchical nature of interpersonal relationships but may also increase the negotiating potential of users to challenge these hierarchies. While technological advances, such as the Internet and mobile communications, have enabled migrants to seek opportunities farther away, this has multiplied the potential for family members to "reach out to those abroad with infinite demands and expectations" (Nyamnjoh 2005: 260). Indeed one of the primary reasons for owning a cell phone is to be able to enforce migrants' obligations to provide financial assistance and modern

---

[53] Interview with Gregory at his home in Capricorn (15 September 2012).

consumer goods (Nyamnjoh 2005: 243). For some such migrants, constant harassment can leave them feeling underappreciated, overwhelmed, and sometimes broke (see field notes excerpt 'Gregory's Buzz' on the following page).

Gregory's Buzz [54]

[Gregory's phone started to ring but he ignored it]

P: Don't mind me Gregory, answer if you need to.

G: [twists his hand flippantly without looking at the phone] No, it's a buzz.

P: A buzz? Like a 'please call me'?

G: [laughs and nods] Yes just to alert me that I must call.

P: Who was calling?

G: It's my cousin. Actually he's the son of the uncle that I'm just telling you about. The one who was in Cape Town and living here. He runs a church in Malawi. Well he is trying to.

G: So what do you think he is calling about?

P: He wants money I think because they are trying to pay for their house and start up their church, my uncle and his new wife, and my cousin is helping them also. Whatever I save I give a little bit.... I must think about these things because these calls will come sometime.

P: And what about saving for yourself Gregory? [I laughed] Who thinks about that, hey?

G: [laughs hard and shakes his head profusely] Well no one Paula, not even me, I can't even think about it. But God is good. I can call on God for help.

P: Do people in Malawi think you are rich?

G: [laughs and thinks deeply for a moment] well I think they

---

[54] Conversation on 15 September 2012.

know I am not rich but they also think us in South Africa are making lots of money. Some of them know what it is like here, like my uncle but most of them not. And even my Uncle, he knows but he still depends on me. It's hard there.

P: And do you correct people? Do you tell them what it is really like in South Africa?

G: [shakes his head profusely] No, no I can't. I always just say ok as soon as I can I will send something. Like my cousin needs new glasses because his vision is poor. I can't send the money now but I have been putting away and I just reassure him that it is coming, it is coming.

Gregory indicated in our conversation that the tensions of being called upon for support from home is mediated by the possibility to "call on God" at any time. Goliama (2010: 178) notes that the power to converse instantaneously and across time and space was once reserved for God. Today, due to mobile technology, anyone can achieve the power of presence in many places simultaneously. The cell phone has given humans the power to converse instantaneously and across distances and to maintain perpetual contact in a godlike fashion (Goliama 2010: 179). This, Goliama (2010: 179) argues, only serves to enhance believers' view of God: "If humans can hardly shake off the searching power of the cell phone, an artefact made with their own hands, what about the searching power of God?" Observing Gregory's use of Facebook to share religious messages and prayers I joked with him that maybe God also had Facebook. He laughed but also stressed that God sees everything. He hears your prayers even if they are quiet. Yet his use of Facebook to 'contact' God signified that actively remaining in contact with God is important. Gregory posted a message on Facebook directly to Jesus: "Thank you my Jesus for everything that happened to my life good or bad I think you have a purpose for everything although there are other things which I still can't forget them because I still feel pain and not guilt. Bless Him forever."[55] It is not possible to hide one's true nature from God (Goliama 2010: 197) but Facebook mediates this by facilitating contact, prayer and good wishes.

Goliama (2010: xiii) contends that the cell phone as a communication tool also "offers the possibility for that medium to become a tool that affords people's openness to God." Features of the Facebook posts for God on Daisy (a 33-year old woman from Malawi) and Gregory's pages included words of encouragement such as "Jesus will never let you down!", "The Lord is my saviour and he is always there for me", or more direct appeals to God such as "God be on my side I beg you please. Let the Devil be ashamed!" or the use of Psalms calling to God for attention and to persuade him to heed the call such as "In Jesus name, I bind you Satan and all your agents from my dreams! Bring every thought, every imagination, and every dream into the captivity and obedience of Jesus Christ (Ps. 16:7-9)". The mobile culture, Goliama (2010: xi) argues, sends a message that one is perpetually available to God. Calling on God arises in part out of the belief that devotion persuades God to act. Although God hears everything, devotion to prayer is seen as the best way to ensure prosperity in the Pentecostal church (Horton 1994: 520-521). As Joseph has said, "You have to serve God. We have to pray and ask and communicate. It is not a one-sided relationship you see."[56]

---

55 Posted on Facebook (2 January 2013).
56 Interview with Gregory and Joseph at Gregory's home in Capricorn (24 November 2012).

Inter-subjective Agency and Migrant Identity Construction: Facebook and the Cell Phone

"Hoped-for Possible Selves"[57] in a Hoped-for Possible Cape Town

My conversation with Gregory (see 'Gregory's Buzz') elucidated important considerations with regards to the perception of migrants' financial situation in South Africa and the way migrants portray their lives to people back home via Facebook. Nyamnjoh (2005) describes the extension of Nyongo witchcraft in relation to migration among the Grassfields people of Cameroon. A person is accused of Nyongo witchcraft when he or she is believed to have taken the life essence of another person through a "temporary death" (Nyamnjoh 2005: 242). The practitioner of Nyongo benefits by using the temporarily dead victim as a slave, or zombie. Today, young migrants increasingly perceive themselves as zombified victims of Nyongo due to the excessive demands placed on them to send home modern goods. This results in an ambivalent sense of belonging, neither wanted at home except for the material possessions they bring, and not entirely welcome in their host countries. Although Gregory reassured me that family members call to "just say hello", he emphasised that a lack of understanding about the situation in South Africa often made him feel isolated. I probed Gregory further as to why he does not inform people what it is really like in South Africa:

"I can't say no because they depend on me. I'm the only one here now from my part of the family. When I go back to Malawi they will also help me. Like when I came here my uncle helped me so

---

[57] In Zhao *et al.* (2008).

now I help him and his sons. Also he took care of me when I was young...We must look after each other." [58]

While Gregory's answer emphasised his role as a provider and his strong interdependent ties to familial networks, his Facebook profile also indicated that pride is a factor in the way that he portrays his life in South Africa. As part of a broader *mediascape* of images that inform perceptions of the world (Appadurai 1990), Facebook images may inform perceptions and hopes attached to other places. Gregory's Facebook profile comprised posts encouraging his favourite football team, Manchester United; posts related to God; and pictures of himself in different parts of Cape Town such as the beach and waterfront. Chalfen (1991: 167) contends that all people taking photographs are selective and purposeful as "personal photography encourages us to establish identities as individuals...who inevitably have relationships to social groupings, personal affiliations, and cultural memberships."

Zhao *et al.* (2008: 1828) posit that Facebook users construct and assert an identity based on their "hoped-for possible self". In his work among societies of the savannah region of northern Togo, Piot describes a grim post-Cold War state, defined for the new generation as exclusion from the global order and a rejection of old authority structures (Piot 2010: 62-63; 54; 105; 166; 167). In this context there has been an attempt to detach from the past and redefine a new, modern world order, a yearning which Piot (2010: 63) terms a "nostalgia for the future". This utopian longing finds expression in membership with Pentecostal churches which emphasise supernatural abundance, direct and spontaneous

[58] Interview with Gregory at his home in Capricorn (15 September 2012)

connection with God, a personal and historical break with the past, and a trans-local Christian identity. New subjectivities also form in this context, where disruptions in social and family ties, mass migration, urbanisation and displacement are common. With a longing for modernity, previous notions of collective good triumphing over individual self-expression are reversed. Personal development is the pre-condition for social good and development, and is achieved through education, travel and consumption (Piot 2010: 20; 70; 147). Similarly the "hoped-for possible self" portrayed by Gregory and Daisy on Facebook is an attempt to establish a new trans-local identity, partly based in Christianity, and an attempt to attain the benefits of globalisation.

Migrants such as Gregory, Miriam, Joseph and Daisy set out on their own to seek independence and opportunities for self-betterment. While they are also working for the common good of their families, leaving home has given them the freedom to imagine another, possible future self – an independent, abundant self, different from the self that was back home. This is expressed in Facebook with pictures of their 'hoped-for lives' in Cape Town to be seen by those left back home. I probed Gregory as to why he does not put "more realistic" pictures up on Facebook. He laughed and responded:

"I can't do that! Ok in Malawi everyone thinks they will come to South Africa and just get rich. And it's killing us here, killing our pockets, that they don't know how it is. But even if I told them they wouldn't believe me. They want hope for the future. I also had those hopes and so I got here." [59]

---

[59] Interview with Gregory at his home in Capricorn (15 September 2012).

Home: A Negotiation of Past and Future

Migration presents several contradictions for migrants. Like many of the migrants I spent time with, Lisa negotiated complex feelings of hope and disappointment, of wanting to belong and wanting to go home, and of seeking new opportunities while also taking positions and accepting living standards that did not reflect her level of education or professional dreams.

Lisa, who has been in Cape Town for four years, described her experience of leaving Zimbabwe for South Africa, a place she had only heard of from fellow Zimbabweans and television:

> "...*We didn't expect it to be like this. I mean you see images of South Africa on TV and we had heard about it but when you get to Capricorn and say ah this is where I will be living it's a shock at first. And rents are high even for this [*waves her hand around the small living space*]... We live in brick houses [at home] and there is more space... At home I was working for a business. I studied accounting and my father ran a business. I am educated. But here I am a domestic worker... But the economy is so bad there ... My son is still there because it is safer for him. ...Also there he can be with family... Of course we would rather be there too. It's home. But we can't right now."* [60]

My conversation with Lisa indicated that coming to Cape Town represented a future in which much hope is invested. Gregory emphasised the financial burdens of being in Cape Town and having to send money home, but his use of Facebook indicated that portraying a self that has 'made it' was important. Gregory admitted that his portrayal of Cape

---

Town, the 'future' is skewed but that it gives people hope, which is more important. Gregory and Lisa both told me that they would rather be at home, but are in South Africa for economic reasons. They plan to achieve enough success in Cape Town to return home with a financial base.

Ferguson (1999) describes the maintenance of rural ties (by meeting social and financial demands) by Copperbelt mineworkers who saw their rural homes as 'traditional' and 'backward' but also insurance in the face of the disappointments of modernity and migration in the late 1980s. With the expectations of modernity dashed, migration was often a case of moving away from the Copperbelt, back to rural areas, rather than migrating to it. Rural areas became "not so much as a remembered past... but an anticipated future." (Ferguson 1999: 165). Similarly, Meyer (1998: 336-337) describes the struggle that emerges among new adherents to Pentecostalism as they are pulled between a notion of personhood and identity which is based on being part of a family and the desire to be a modern person living an independent life. This conflict stems from concrete pressures from extended family as well as guilt over indulging in an individualist lifestyle which is counter to traditional family-oriented values. Emotional ties to home and family were major factors in maintaining connections, as reflected by Lisa's comments. The desire to return home may be further complicated when the children of migrants feel more at home in Cape Town than their parents, as has happened with Diana and Tendai's children. As Ferguson (1999: 82) claims, "the path" "back"... is thus neither automatic nor easy."

Parallels can be drawn between the idea of the past, as symbolised by 'back home' and the future, represented by migration to Cape Town, with discourses around modernisation and development. Joseph rarely sends money home; he doesn't plan to return and he is relatively disconnected from family. As he has emphasised, home is *"where there is a move of the spirit."*[61] Joseph's more indistinct notion of home and desire to follow opportunities into new spaces as opposed to returning to Malawi reflects a cosmopolitanism that Englund (2004: 296) argues emerges "when there is unease or uncertainty about the 'home' that most immediately imposes itself upon the subject." Joseph and Miriam are close friends and have likely connected due to their commitment to independence and freedom of movement. For Miriam, somewhat alienated from home due to different religious beliefs and since the death of her mother, home as a place inside herself connected to God is more desirable. In Mpumalanga she belongs but also feels alien; in Cape Town she belongs as a South African but as a Zulu woman living alone she is perceived as foreign. Miriam and Joseph's cosmopolitanism is generated not just from an inherent openness but a renegotiation of belonging beyond geographical terms, "in favour of home as a set of comforting practises and relationships" (Nyamnjoh 2005: 243).

Within "expectations of modernity" (Ferguson 1999) lies an implicit presumption of a break with the past. Yet ICTs are also used by those 'back home' to connect the past with the present and to keep pace with modernity and future possibilities. This would suggest that dichotomies around modernisation as a linear progression are inappropriate in light of migrants' negotiation of relationships with people back home and in Cape Town. Most of Gregory's Facebook friends are home connections. In fact a significant portion of Gregory's Facebook profile is taken up by posts from friends

---

[61] Interview with Joseph at his home in Capricorn (23 August 2012).

and family in Malawi sharing major events such as birthdays and weddings. Their posts also reflect their "hoped-for possible selves" (Zhao *et al.* 2008: 1828). Facebook is one of the main forums Gregory and Daisy use for 'keeping in touch' as it is less expensive than phoning or texting and always accessible through the Facebook phone application. Gregory also revealed that Facebook tends to be more social and less urgent.[62] This would suggest that while 'back home' is seen as the past, the past is also catching up with the present. Although the view of the future is skewed, people at home have the opportunity to sustain contact with their migrant friends and family. Thus the modern becomes traditionalised and tradition becomes modernised. The traditional-modern, past-future, rural-urban dichotomies are negotiated and in such a way that the future can be seen to be catching up with the present and the past (see Nyamnjoh 2003).

Ferguson (1999: 85) argues against the "narrative of an emerging urban modernity set against the dark background of a static rural tradition..." Although he concedes that this dualism was also part of the narrative of Copperbelt mineworkers in Zambia who spoke of themselves as "suspended between two worlds –one modern...and another rural, traditional", he encourages scholars to move away from conceptions of Africa as developing in a linear progressive sequence to capture the "multitudinous coexisting variations" (Ferguson 1999: 42) of strategies for straddling urban-rural connections among migrants disenchanted with modernisation. As Meyer (1998: 329; 332) highlights with regards to Pentecostalism's emphasis on a discontinuity with

---

[62] Interview with Gregory and Joseph at Gregory's home in Capricorn (24 November 2012).

the past, the stress on breaking with the past does not necessarily entail a total dismissal. The past becomes part of the ritual practise which involves moving back and forth between both in order to justify the gap between aspirations and actual, often unfavourable, circumstances. Meyer (1998: 332) writes that a dialectic relationship with evil spirits makes it possible to become aware of one's links with tradition and family and therefore become modern by "remembering in order to forget". She writes: "Pentecostal discourse about rupture allows members not only to approach the ideal of modern, individual identity, but also to address those ties which they seek to leave behind but which still matter in their lives." (Meyer 1998: 332)

Conclusion

In this chapter I have argued that ICTs allow migrants to connect relatively instantly with people at home and in their host countries, but that the obstacles related to connectivity and physical boundaries mean that distance cannot be entirely overcome. Furthermore, the pervasiveness of the technology can also cause problems with regards to unwanted communication. Migrants may be inundated with requests from family and friends back home to send money. The tensions of being called upon for support from home, however, may be mediated by the possibility to 'call on God'. Being devoted to God gives believers the privilege of persuading God to act, and ICTs such as Facebook are implicated in this as appeals and prayers to God can be sent immediately by posting on Facebook or sending text messages.

ICTs are implicated in the bridging and bonding capital provided by membership at the Bay. Membership can facilitate alternative notions of kinship – as fellow worshipers can all be considered 'brothers and sisters in Christ.' This is highly relevant in the context of migration where more supportive relationships can be found amongst fellow migrants with similar experiences or fellow church members with similar religious identities. Kinship and associated roles and expectations must also be negotiated in order to maintain conviviality. The cell phone allows for a negotiation of intimacy and distance with the option to call or text message depending on the nature of the interaction, and the intimacy or distance required such as in requesting prayers or financial assistance.

ICTs are implicated in migrants' emphasis on their identities as Christians and as successful migrants. The "hoped-for possible self" (Zhao *et al.* 2008: 1828) portrayed by Gregory and Daisy on Facebook is an attempt to establish a trans-local identity, partly based in Christianity. These posts communicate important terms for belonging at home and abroad. Pentecostalism has been characterised by its promotion of a discontinuity with what has come before (see Anderson *et al.* 2010: 160). However, a focus only on the rhetoric of Pentecostalism, similar to modernisation discourses that emphasise linear development, detracts from the actions and interactions of people towards conviviality between the past and the present in the interest of the future.

Chapter 5

Conclusion:
A Reflection on Research Findings and
Multi-Spaces Anthropological Fieldwork

My research sought to address how migrants form and maintain convivial relationships at the Bay Community Church in Cape Town and how these relationships are facilitated by ICTs. I argued that migrants establish convivial relationships with family members back home and fellow church members in Cape Town by negotiating intimacy and distance. I further argued that ICTs can facilitate intimacy but also provide the capacities to mitigate this with distance. In forming and maintaining convivial relationships, this capacity for distance can be imperative. In the context of multi-spaces ethnographic research, the use of the mobile phone brought up questions with regards to the changing field of anthropology and how anthropologists can adapt.

This conclusion comprises: a) a summary of the main conclusions of this book, organised according to chapter; b) a discussion of how and to what extent my findings have answered my initial research question; c) a reflection on how the many subject positions implicated in friendships with participants illuminated some of the challenges of participatory and democratic knowledge production; and d) a consideration of the potential in, and value of moving beyond traditional researcher-subject positions in the interest of more accommodating models of knowledge production.

Summary Conclusions

In Chapter One, I provided a background to the research, emphasizing that migrants have managed to overcome structural exclusion and xenophobia by establishing convivial relationships in Cape Town. I conceptualised conviviality as an inter-subjective process of amicably balancing intimacy and distance. This conceptualisation was useful for exploring migrants' negotiation of past and future, animosity and friendship, being an insider and an outsider, and individual desires and family obligations. I argued that dichotomies such as these are ultimately problematic when the experience of migration involves such a creative adoption of innovations and strategies, each with their own possibilities and limitations depending on the unique position and habitus of the individual.

In Chapter Two, I explored the challenges and opportunities of multi-spaces fieldwork and the possibilities of overcoming common researcher-subject divides. Unlike anthropologists who go into the field at a distant location away from home for a continuous period of time, my field spaces were close to home and I spent time in and out of the field, negotiating the terms of being a researcher, friend, insider and outsider with my informants. In this context, the mobile phone was an important mediator as I could be in the field virtually when I was not there physically. Furthermore, developing friendships with my research participants required a personal negotiation of intimacy and distance, and accessibility, in order to reconcile the tension between being an objective bystander and a subjective social person making an impact in the field (Malkki 2007: 177). The intersection and complementarity between virtual and physical presence highlighted in this chapter offers insights and possibilities for conceptualising and innovatively operationalising ethnographic research.

In Chapter Three, I investigated the nature and extent of conviviality at the Bay. I concluded that the intimate nature of interactions at the Bay is facilitated by the style of Charismatic worship. I also concluded that at the Bay, being a Christian was the most powerful criteria for inclusion and was the basis from which to strive for conviviality. The emphasis on a Christian as opposed to national identity enabled migrants to establish a transnational identity and draw on a "transnational habitus" (Gielies 2009: 603). Migrants are able to draw on their habitus as Christians due to their familiarity with Pentecostal styles of worship. This may be done consciously and unconsciously (Owen 2011: 187) but differences in habitus may require a negotiation on the part of migrants and locals in the church context in order to maintain conviviality. I highlighted that habitus is not solely a result of agency or structure but an interplay between the two over time (Bourdieu 1990). Agents may be required to shift their habitus to negotiate changing social fields.

I emphasised that networks and relationships are not necessarily formed solely for the purpose of gaining social resources. More embodied notions of faith and connection are also part of the choice to join a church or invest in a relationship. Spiritual capital, as Stark and Finke (2000) contend, is acquired through emotional and spiritual experiences in particular religious contexts and through particular rituals. I further concluded that the negotiation of past and future, home and away, are implicated in the formation and maintenance of convivial relationships, as migrants must choose where to focus their loyalties and carefully sustain multiple identities and loyalties in order to belong at home and in Cape Town (Levitt 2007: 848). Findings in this chapter suggest the need for future research on the intersection between conviviality and the embodied aspects of religious experience in the context of migration.

In Chapter Four, I investigated the role of ICTs, namely cell phones and Facebook, in facilitating convivial relationships for migrants. I highlighted that the possibility of perpetual contact through the cell phone means outsiders can enjoy interconnectedness, accessibility and the security of personal contact with their loved ones. The absence of their immediate and physically intimate presence, however, can be frustrating and lead to an extension of kinship to fellow worshippers who are all 'brothers and sisters in Christ'. Christian kinship and associated roles and expectations must also be reconciled. In this context, the cell phone allows for a negotiation of intimacy and distance with the option to call or text message depending on the nature of the interaction and the intimacy or distance required such as in requesting prayers or financial assistance. I further argued that followers view ICTs as a medium for accessing God as spiritual thoughts and feelings are communicated and received through technology. This chapter offers a contribution to literature on material culture in terms of the way technology and virtual communication affects bodily practises and embodied esoteric experiences in both senders and receivers.

Research Findings

Religion and Migration: Constructing Identities and Convivial Relationships

Migration presents several contradictions for migrants and requires a negotiation of complex feelings of expectation and disillusionment. While Cape Town symbolises hope and the future, migrants may find themselves disenchanted by their dreams upon arrival. The bold and lonely act of migration can ultimately reinforce social obligations; migrants may find themselves negotiating their individual desires with expectations from home. Gupta and Ferguson (1992) suggest that people's identities are less fixed than anthropology may have earlier suggested. However, they also highlight that people living away from home may also emphasise, as do their hosts, particular identities related to home and 'homeland' in the face of insecurities around the 'other' and a loss of authenticity. Although many of the migrants that participated in this study emphasised that they would prefer to be home, and remain in South Africa for financial reasons, they have clustered around the idea of being at home anywhere due to their Christian identity. Gregory and Daisy's use of Facebook was a testament to the emphasis that they place on their Christian identities above other identities. The portrayal of themselves as devout Christians, like the portrayal of their lives in Cape Town are idealised (see Zhou et al. 2008), however they communicate desires about belonging both at home and abroad, particularly being 'brothers and sisters in Christ' (see Aasgaard 2004) and 'at home and one in Christ.' [63]

---

[63] Interview with Joseph at his home in Capricorn (23 August 2012).

At the outset, migration and Pentecostalism both present opportunities for breaking with the past. However, the past also becomes part of the ritual practise which involves moving back and forth between both in order to justify the gap between aspirations and actual, often unfavourable, circumstances (Meyer 1998). Migrants use the past, represented by the traditional spiritual beliefs of their families, as a marker against which to assert their Christian identities. Home itself also represents the past (see Ferguson 1999) and migrants assert their identities as successful individuals, having achieved the future desires of many at home. As Levitt (2002: 848) argues, transnational identities are formed out of both memory and imagination. I highlighted that Facebook offers the potential to portray one's ideal, "hoped-for self" (Zhou *et al.* 2008) and is implicated in the negotiation of identities that emphasise religious rebirth and success in Cape Town, portrayed against the 'past' of back home.

The role of religion in the construction or strengthening of national or ethnic identities, customs and language for immigrants is emphasised in literature on religion and migration (Cadge and Hecklund 2007: 363; Ebaugh and Chafetz 2000). While Levitt (2007: 848) highlights that migrants keep their feet in two worlds simultaneously by belonging to transnational religious organisations, she emphasises that these organisations tend to reinforce migrants' attachments to home. This book has highlighted the ways in which religious and national identities are expressed in diverse ways simultaneously (see also Ng 2002). Joseph read Malawian news on the internet at work and Gregory maintained close friendships with Malawians in his residential area in order to "feel that I am connected with my people."[64] However, I emphasised that migrants accentuate their transnational religious identity over their national identities in order to belong in many worlds at once. Lisa highlighted the importance of belonging to a church with a diverse congregation for maintaining convivial relationships and networks as opposed to remaining in close knit nationally-based networks that can become so intimate as to be rendered oppressive.

Although Pentecostalism emphasises a break from family traditions and the importance of individual salvation (Meyer 1998), maintaining convivial relationships and emotional ties to home requires that migrants negotiate their individual interests with familial obligations and demands. This is a tentative balance however, and familial obligations often take precedence (see Chen 2005). Although individual desires are carefully negotiated to maintain support systems in the eventuality of return to home, such social pressure can add a heavy weight to the stresses of everyday life. Gregory for example, participates in family traditions despite his religious beliefs because he does not want to upset anyone. Although on one level he participates in order to maintain a sense of belonging at home, this causes internal strife, which the group does not see.

An important theme in this book has been the role of agency in migrants' identity construction. The importance of individual salvation plays into many migrants' experiences of setting off on their own in an attempt to ameliorate their socio-economic status (Meyer 1998). Ng (2002) highlights the role of agency in establishing religious identities, suggesting that approaching religion solely as a bridge for migrants can detract from an understanding of how non-traditional

---

[64] Interview with Joseph at his home in Capricorn (11 August 2012).

religions are taken up (Ng 2002: 3). While Gregory joined the Bay because it was where his uncle attended, migrants such as Miriam and Lisa chose to move away from traditional spiritual beliefs or predominantly migrant churches in order to form new and different connections.

There is also a gendered aspect to migrants' decisions to join religious organisations, as highlighted by Meyer (1998). Miriam and two of her church friends Andiswa and Ilse, for example, are single women striving to move upward socio-economically. Women, Meyer (1998) contends, join Pentecostal churches to seek support and independence from male-dominated power structures. This book highlighted that women such as Miriam and Lisa make choices to join particular religious institutions as part of their drive to be economically independent and successful. Scholars of immigrant religion have generally concluded that immigrant religion tends to reinforce traditional patriarchy (see Ebaugh and Chafetz 2000; Yang 2004), but literature on immigration and gender more broadly suggests that women gain independence through immigration due to their greater access to educational opportunities and because of the necessity of a women's financial contribution to the family (see Chen 2005).[65]

ICTs as a Medium for Conviviality

The proliferation of cell phone technology and the massive following of Christianity, particularly Pentecostalism, in Africa calls for a critical analysis of the role of ICTs in

---

[65] In terms of remittances, female migrants generally earn less and send a greater proportion of their income than men. Women also generally send money more regularly than men (IOM and UN-INSTRAW 2007: 2).

shaping relationships among religious believers. Both religion and cell phones are relevant to the negotiation of marginality as both have ambivalent implications for migrants' insider-outsider status. For example, Miriam's messages of conversion to her non-religious family outside of Cape Town, highlighted the way that mobile cultures blur social borders and shape relationships in new ways. In doing so Miriam also asserted her identity as a Christian against a family of non-believers and simultaneously, filled herself with Jesus' light in spreading His word. The immediacy of communication that cell phones provide also has implications for users' ability to serve God (Goliama 2010: xi). Being devoted to God gives believers the privilege of persuading God to act, and ICTs facilitate an immediate connection by being able to post prayers on Facebook or sending text messages requesting prayers from fellow church members. The belief of having immediate access to God through Facebook can further mediate the tensions and loneliness of being inundated with calls from home requesting financial support. The past, represented by the traditional spiritual beliefs of families, is also used as a marker against which to assert one's Christian identities. This negotiation of past, present and future is facilitated by ICTs.

This work has highlighted the implications of religious belonging for migrants but also the implications of the physical aspects of worship on belonging and convivial relationships. Relationships between worshippers were shaped by identification with Jesus and the incorporation of Jesus into the body container. Bodies and subjectivities were shaped by ritual, which brought about spontaneous, intimate and convivial interactions (see Warnier 2009: 419-420). In her work on religious conversion among Taiwanese women,

Chen (2005: 14) gives a brief example of the calming effect of chanting and how this impacted one woman's relationship with her mother-in-law. Griffith highlights that religious converts have also described their experiences as liberating and a recovery of their authentic selves (1997: 104). I drew on Goliama (2011) and Warnier (2006; 2009) to further consider how the cell phone can be a medium for accessing God. Warnier's (2006; 2009) work was useful in considering how spiritual thoughts and feelings are communicated through technology and how they are transformed and received. Spiritual texts, prayers, and words of encouragement can be communicated via text message or Facebook. These in turn may affect a bodily reaction for the person on the other end – they may feel the presence of God or feel motivated to pray. Thus matters of the spirit are extended into the tool through the act of communicating about them. A focus on the embodiment of religious worship and cell phone use has highlighted the biological and cognitive constraints on human emotion and experience that reduce differences between people and between researchers and subjects.

Cell phones are often perceived as being either synonymous with progress and development or as a form of capitalist exploitation ruinous to African traditions (Nkwi 2009: 51). Recent anthropological work on ICTs and society (De Bruijn *et al.* 2009: 88, Molony 2007 and van Binsbergen 2004) suggests that ICTs are appropriated and interpreted locally in unique ways. Brinkman et al. (2009: 79) highlight that cell phones can create intimacy and distance between people. For example, they can facilitate relationships among young people of the opposite sex, but parents may feel distanced from their children who they perceive to be committing subterfuge with their secretive use of mobile phones. Horst and Miller (2006: 83) similarly highlight that cell phones can assist in the coordination of activities and maintenance of networks but that the inconsistent, layered nature of networks must be accounted for. Networks are formed through reciprocity but also contain deceptions. I further argued that while cell phones may allow for an expansion of networks, distance is equally implicated in the expansion and negotiation of networks, especially in a community like the Bay. Thus the cell phone is a device which connects but "whose importance lies in its capacity to keep multiple strands separate" (Horst and miller 2006: 83). Mobile phones are used to expand networks by providing instant, affordable connection just as much as they may have to be used to manage intimacy through screening calls or using text messaging functions at appropriate moments. Both cell phones and religion have the potential to challenge traditional socially constructed divides that have usually distanced socio-economic classes and different ethnic groups.

Fieldwork: Negotiating Friendships and the Role of ICTs

Through fieldwork I sought to understand how anthropologists can overcome researcher-subject divides towards more democratic knowledge production. As migrants' stories of movement were characterised by the crossing of spatial and cultural borders it was important that my fieldwork was not spatially bounded. I explored the challenges and opportunities of multi-spaces fieldwork. The migrants involved in my research negotiated the boundaries of belonging in Cape Town through their belief in God and through ICTs. I, therefore, had to consider how to capture shared esoteric as well as virtual experiences as part of my fieldwork.

Gupta and Ferguson (1997) contend that the field should not be seen as a distinct and bounded place but an interconnected space in which place and identities are negotiated. My fieldwork primarily took place in migrants' homes in Capricorn Township and at the Bay Community Church. Although my fieldwork was not multi-sited in that it took place in the same city, I conducted fieldwork in many spaces by following people and concepts to different locations. Marcus (1995: 102) argues that as the object of a single study is "ultimately mobile and multiply situated". Tracing the movement of products, knowledge, and connections is highly relevant when culture is considered a process, as opposed to a static state of affairs (Coleman and von Hellerman 2002: 168). In widening one's focus to many sites, however the anthropologist may lose the nuances of the everyday local level (Coleman and von Hellermann 2012: 169). Although my time at church events outside of the Bay was limited, my informants remained the same. My focus was to observe and investigate the way informants behaved and felt in different spaces, particularly various churches, giving me greater insight into their networks, religious experiences, and the role of the Bay in their lives. Participant observation in this sense can also entail spending time and observing the same individuals in many spaces as opposed to focusing on a bounded space.

I conducted fieldwork in cyberspace by communicating with my informants over the phone and through text messages and Facebook. Facebook proved to be a field space in its own right because of the ways in which migrants used it to construct identities that contradicted things they said.

102

Gregory, for example complained about people in Malawi being unaware of what life in Cape Town is really like. However, his use of Facebook to emphasise having 'made it' contradicted this view. Observing and interacting with Gregory and Daisy on Facebook was a form of participant observation and I remained 'in the field' virtually, as well as physically.

Conducting fieldwork in the virtual world enables the construction of connections between spaces and can also be conceptualised as a distinct field space. I took heed of Gupta and Ferguson's (1992:8) suggestion that 'community' may refer to a delimited physical space but can also refer to "clusters of interaction". Considering 'cyberspace' as clusters of human interaction, it can also be seen as a space in its own right and one which might link other spaces. My mobile phone was also instrumental in making appointments with participants who would otherwise not have had access to land lines or internet for email. Conducting fieldwork 'at home' and using my cell phone in the context of research caused distance as I was not always required to negotiate "the vagaries of chance" but phone calls or text messages from participants also delivered useful data and were instrumental in forming connections and maintaining relationships in the field (Pelckmans 2009: 28).

Reflections on Friendships and Being 'Buzzed' in the Field

Anthropology has come far in terms of overcoming disciplinary tendencies towards reinforcing extreme otherness in its portrayals. Owen (2011), for example, describes falling in love with one of her participants, capturing the complexity of researcher-subject relationships. In my fieldwork, becoming friends with my participants helped to overcome researcher-subject divides as well as divides along the lines of socio-economic status and religious beliefs. It also enabled my participants and me to accommodate each other as unique individuals, rather than people fulfilling roles. As a result, I also realised the extent to which my data shifted and even became contradictory. This highlighted that I was not an authoritative outsider and that the 'insiders' knowledge should not be taken for granted, and certainly not taken at face value. Still, issues around trust and obligation arose which had to be negotiated. For example, in order to balance the use of participants' time for my interests, I often felt obliged to meet their requests for assistance with transport. As a researcher seeking data, friendship was not the only aim of maintaining relationships with my new friends. I argue that it is important not to romanticise friendships in the field as totally equalising but to be reflexive about the effects of various subject positions on researcher-subject relationships and move conscientiously between these subject positions.

Using my mobile phone during research presented interesting dynamics in terms of negotiating intimacy and distance with my informants. Pelckmans (2009) describes 'flashing', or 'buzzing'. The phone user considered to have more money becomes the "credit caretaker" and receives missed calls to which he or she is expected to call back (Pelckmans 2009: 29). Researchers are often considered wealthy and may therefore be subject to flashes, which indeed I was. Flashing practises influence and reproduce power relations among people and the researcher is shaped by these practises (Pelckmans 2009). During fieldwork, being 'buzzed' by informants helped our friendship develop as the cell phone was a medium for socialising more casually when I was not in the field actively seeking data. On the other hand, I also felt pressured to keep in touch frequently due to the regularity of messages from informants.

The use of mobile technology and ICTs such as Facebook in the context of anthropological research calls for a consideration of how anthropologists approach globalisation and the increased mobility and connectivity of the anthropological subject. Appadurai (2000: 5) addresses the implications of globalisation for the discipline of anthropology and stress the importance of studying "global cultural flows", rather than fixed and bounded "cultures". Anthropologists face the challenge of appropriately approaching the topic of globalisation's flows and dealing with subject matter that is changing and constantly in motion. Globalisation challenges the dichotomy of native and anthropologist. More research as to how cell phones can facilitate co-production of anthropological work could contribute to a democratisation of the knowledge production process.

References

Aasgaard, R. (2004). *My Beloved Brothers and Sisters: Christian Siblingship in Paul* (Vol. 265). New York: Continuum International Publishing Group.

Adichie, C. (2009). "The danger of a single story." TED: Ideas worth spreading. http://www.ted.com/talks/chimamanda_adichie_the_da nger_of_a_single_story.html [accessed 12 October 2013].

African Seer (2013). "Thousands of Zimbabweans flock to South Africa for Pastor Chris Oyakhilome's conference." http://www.africanseer.com/headline/260884-thousands-of-zimbabweans-flock-to-south-africa-for-pastor-chris-oyakhilome-s-conference.html [accessed 25 July 2013].

Albrecht, D.E. (1999). *Rites in the Spirit: A Ritual Approach to Pentecostal/Charismatic Spirituality* (Vol. 17). New York: Continuum International Publishing Group.

Ammerman, N.T. & Farnsley, A.E. (1997). *Congregation & Community*. New Brunswick: Rutgers University Press.

Anderson, A. (2004). *An Introduction to Pentecostalism: Global Charismatic Christianity*. Cambridge: Cambridge University Press.

Anderson, A., Bergunder, M., Droogers, A.F., & Van der Laan, C. (2010). *Studying Global Pentecostalism*. Berkeley: University of California Press.

Appadurai, A. (1990). "Disjuncture and Difference in the Global Cultural Economy." *Cultural Theory: An Anthology.* Eds. I. Szwman & T. Kaposy. West Sussex: Wiley-Blackwell. 282-295.

Appadurai, A. (2000). "Grassroots Globalization and the Research Imagination." *Public Culture*, 12(1), 1-19.

Beer, B. (2001). "Anthropology of Friendship." *International Encyclopedia of the Social and Behavioural Sciences.* Eds. N.J. Smelser & P.B. Baltes. Kidlington: Elsevier, 5805–5808.

Bernard, H.R. (2006). *Research Methods in Anthropology: Qualitative and Quantitative Approaches.* Oxford: AltaMira Press.

Bourdieu, P. (1984) *Distinction: a Social Critique of the Judgement of Taste.* London: Routledge & Keegan Paul.

Bourdieu, P. (1986). "Force of Law: Toward a Sociology of the Juridical Field". *The Hastings LJ, 38,* 805.

Bourdieu, P. (1990). *The Logic of Practice.* Stanford: Stanford University Press.

Bourdieu, P. (2004). *Science of Science and Reflexivity.* Cambridge: Polity.

Brinkman, I., de Bruijn, M., Hisham, B. (2009). "The Mobile Phone, 'Modernity' and Change in Khartoum, Sudan." *Mobile Phones: The New Talking Drums of Everyday Africa.*

Eds. M. de Bruijn, F.B. Nyamnjoh & I. Brinkman. Langaa/ASC: Cameroon/ Leiden, 69-91.

Burgess, S.M., & Van der Maas, E.M. (Eds.). (2010). *The New International Dictionary of Pentecostal and Charismatic Movements: Revised and Expanded Edition.* Grand Rapids: Zondervan.

Cadge, W., & Howard Ecklund, E. (2007). "Immigration and Religion." *Annual Review of Sociology*, 33, 359-379.

Callon, M. (1991). "Techno-Economic Networks and Irreversibility." *A Sociology of Monsters: Essays on Power, Technology and Domination*, *38*, 132-161.

Campbell, H. (2005). "Making Space for Religion in Internet Studies." *The Information Society*, *21*(4), 309-315.

Campbell, H. (2005). "The Impact of the Mobile Phone on Young People's Social Life." Paper presented to the Social Change in the 21st Century Conference, Queensland, Australia: Centre for Social Change Research Queensland University of Technology: 28 October 2005.

Candea, M. (2007). "Arbitrary Locations: in Defence of the Bounded Field-site." *Journal of the Royal Anthropological Institute*, 13(1), 167-184.

Castells, M., Fernandez-Ardevol, M., Qui, J.L. & Sey, A. (2004). *The Mobile Communication Society: A cross-cultural analysis of available evidence on the social uses of wireless communication technology.* Los Angeles: Aneneberg Research Network on International Communication.

Castles, S. (2002). "Migration and Community Formation under Conditions of Globalization". *International Migration Review, 36*(4), 1143-1168.

Chalfen, R. (1991). *Turning leaves: the photograph collections of two Japanese American families.* Albuquerque: University of New Mexico Press.

Chen, C. (2005). "A Self of One's Own Taiwanese Immigrant Women and Religious Conversion". *Gender & Society, 19*(3), 336-357.

Clarke, K.M. (2004). *Mapping Yoruba Networks: Power and Agency in the Making of Transnational Communities.* Durham: Duke University Press.

Clarke, K. (2007). "Transnational Yoruba Revivalism and the Diasporic Politics of Heritage". *American Ethnologist, 34*(4), 721-734.

Coleman, J.S. (2000). "Social capital in the creation of human capital". *Knowledge and Social Capital.* Ed. E.L. Lesser. Boston: Butterworth-Heinemann, 17-41.

Coleman, S., & Von Hellermann, P. (Eds.). (2012). *Multi-sited ethnography: problems and possibilities in the translocation of research methods.* Routledge: New York.

Comaroff, J., & Comaroff, J.L. (Eds.). (1993). *Modernity and its Malcontents: Ritual and Power in Postcolonial Africa.* Chicago: University of Chicago Press.

Comaroff, J.L., & Comaroff, J. (2009). *Ethnicity, Inc.* Chicago: University of Chicago Press.

Crush, J. (2008). "South Africa: Policy in the Face of Xenophobia. Migration Information Source: Country Profiles" www.migrationinformation.org/Feature/display.cfm?ID =689 [accessed on 31 August 2012].

Csordas, T. (1999). "Embodiment and Cultural Phenomenology." *Perspectives on Embodiment: The Intersections of Nature and Culture.* Eds. G. Weiss & H. F. Haber. New York/London: Routledge, 143-62.

De Bruijn, M., Nyamnjoh, F.B., & Brinkman, I. (Eds.). (2009). *Mobile Phones: The New Talking Drums of Everyday Africa.* Cameroon/ Leiden: Langaa/ASC.

Delanty, G. (2000). *Citizenship in a Global Age: Society, Culture, Politics.* Buckingham: Open University Press.

Duponchel, M. (2013). "Who's the Alien? Xenophobia in Post-apartheid South Africa." *United Nations University-WIDER Working Paper,* 003

Ebaugh, H.R.F., & Chafetz, J.S. (Eds.). (2002). *Religion Across Borders: Transnational Immigrant Networks.* Walnut Creek, California: AltaMira Press.

Englund, H. (2003). "Christian Independency and Global Membership: Pentecostal Extraversions in Malawi". *Journal of Religion in Africa*, 33(1), 83-111.

Englund, H. (2004). "Cosmopolitanism and the Devil in Malawi." *Ethnos*, 69(3), 293-316.

Ferguson, J. (1999). *Expectations of Modernity: Myths and Meanings of Urban Life on the Zambian Copperbelt.* Berkeley: University of California Press.

Finke, R. (2003). "Spiritual Capital: Definitions, Applications, and New Frontiers." *Presentation for the Spiritual Capital Planning Meeting, Cambridge, MA, 9-10 October 2003.* http://www.metanexus.net/archive/spiritualcapitalresearchprogram/pdf/finke.pdf [accessed 24 April 2013].

Foley, M.W., McCarthy, J.D., Chaves, M. (2001) "Social Capital, Religious Institutions, and Poor Communities". *Social Capital and Poor Communities.* Eds. S. Saegert, J.P. Thompson, M.R. Warren. New York: Russell Sage Foundation, 215-245.

Fonchingong, T.N. (2010). "The Cell Phone and the Nigerian Immigrants in Anglophone Cameroon". Presentation at the "Mobile Africa Revisited" Workshop, Leiden. 9-10 December 2010.

Geertz, C. (1973). *The Interpretation of Cultures: Selected Essays* (Vol. 5019). New York: Basic books.

Geertz, C. (1998). "Deep Hanging Out." *The New York Review of Books*, 45(16), 69-72.

Gelderblom, D., & Adams, W. (2006). "The Limits and Possibilities of Migrant Networks", *Migration in South and Southern Africa: Dynamics and Determinants*. Eds. P. Kok, D. Gelderblom, J.O. Oucho, J. & Van Zyl. Cape Town: HSRC Publishers, 227-248.

Gielis, R. (2009). "Borders Make the Difference: Migrant Transnationalism as a Border Experience." *Tijdschrift voor economische en sociale geografie*, 100(5), 598-609.

Glick Schiller, N., Basch, L., & Blanc, C.S. (1995). "From Immigrant to Transmigrant: Theorizing Transnational Migration". *Anthropological Quarterly*, 68(1), 48-63.

Glick Schiller, N., Çaglar, A., & Guldbrandsen, T.C. (2006). "Beyond the Ethnic Lens: Locality, Globality, and Born-again Incorporation". *American Ethnologist*, 33(4), 612-633.

Goggin, G. (2012). *Cell phone Culture: Mobile Technology in Everyday Life*. London: Routledge.

Goliama, C.M. (2010). *Where are You Africa?: Church and Society in the Mobile Phone Age*. Oxford: African Books Collective.

Griffith, R. M. (1997). *God's Daughters: Evangelical Women and the Power of Submission*. Berkeley: University of California Press.

Gupta, A., & Ferguson, J. (1992). "Beyond "Culture": Space, Identity, and the Politics of Difference". *Cultural Anthropology*, 7(1), 6-23.

Gupta, A., & Ferguson, J. (Eds.) (1997). "Discipline and practice: "The field" as Site, Method, and Location in Anthropology." *Anthropological Locations: Boundaries and Grounds of a Field Science*, Berkeley: University of California Press.

Hannerz, U. (1989). "Notes on the Global Ecumene". *Public Culture*, 1(2), 66-75.

Hinchliffe, S. & Whatmore, S. (2006). "Living in Cities: Towards a Politics of Conviviality". *Science as Culture* (Special Issue: Technonatural time-spaces), 15 (2), 123-138.

Hollenweger, W.J. (1997). *Pentecostalism: Origins and Developments Worldwide*. Peabody, MA: Hendrickson Publishers.

Horst, H., & Miller, D. (2006). *The cell phone: An Anthropology of Communication*. Oxford/ New York: Berg Publishers.

Horton, S.M. (Ed). (1994). *Systematic Theology: A Pentecostal Perspective*. Springfield, Missouri: Logion Press/Gospel Publishing House.

Human Sciences Research Council (HSRC) (2008.) *Citizenship, Violence and Xenophobia in South Africa: Perceptions from South African Communities*, Democracy and Governance

Programme HSRC: June 2008 http://www.hsrc.ac.za/Document-2807.phtml [accessed 27 February 2012].

Iannaccone, L.R. (1990). "Religious Practice: A Human Capital Approach". *Journal for the Scientific Study of Religion*, 29, 297-314.

International Organization for Migration (IOM) and United Nations International Research and Training Institute for the Advancement of Women (UN-INSTRAW) (2007). "Survey on Remittances 2007: Gender Perspectives". *Working Books on Migration*, 24.

Jenkins, R. (1996) *Social Identity*. London: Routledge.

Kok, P.C. (Ed.). (2006). *Migration in South and Southern Africa: dynamics and determinants*. Cape Town: HSRC Press.

Kopytoff, I. (Ed.). (1987). *The African Frontier: The Reproduction of Traditional African Societies*. Bloomington: Indiana University Press.

Landau, L.B. (2001). "Immigration, Xenophobia and Human Rights in South Africa." *Migration Policy Series*, 22.

Landau, L. & Segatti, A. (2011). *Contemporary Migration to South Africa: A Regional Development Issue*. Washington, D.C./ Paris: World Bank/ Agence Française de Développement.

Landau, L.B. (2012). *Exorcising the Demons Within: Xenophobia, Violence and Statecraft in Contemporary South Africa.* Johannesburg: Wits University Press.

Latour, B. (2005). *Reassembling the Social-An Introduction to Actor-Network-Theory,* Oxford: Oxford University Press.

Leder, D. (1990). *The Absent Body.* Chicago: University of Chicago Press.

Levine, N.E. (2008). "Alternative Kinship, Marriage, and Reproduction". *Annual Review of Anthropology, 37,* 375-389.

Levitt, P. (2002). "Redefining the Boundaries of Belonging: Thoughts on Transnational Religious and Political Life". Working Papers, Centre for Comparative Immigration Studies, UC San Diego. http://ccis.ucsd.edu/wp-content/uploads/2012/08/wrkg48.pdf [accessed 27 February 2012].

Levitt, P. (2007). *God Needs No Passport.* New Press: New York.

Levitt, P., and Glick Schiller, N. (2004). "Conceptualizing Simultaneity: A Transnational Social Field Perspective on Society". *International migration review, 38*(3), 1002-1039.

Lindhardt, M. (Ed.). (2011). *Practicing the Faith: The Ritual Life of Pentecostal-Charismatic Christians.* New York/Oxford: Berghahn Books.

Living Hope (2013). "Capricorn." http://www.livinghope.co.za/about/living-hope/communities/capricorn/ [accessed 25 July 2013].

Luepnitz, D.A. (2002). *Schopenhauer's Porcupines: Dilemmas of Intimacy and the Talking Cure: Five Stories of Psychotherapy.* New York: Basic Books.

Madianou, M. & Miller, D. (2011). "Mobile Phone Parenting: Reconfiguring Relationships between Filipina Migrant Mothers and their Left-behind Children." *New Media and Society*, Vol. 13 (3), pp. 457-470.

Mahler, S.J., & Hansing, K. (2005). "Toward a Transnationalism of the Middle: How Transnational Religious Practices Help Bridge the Divides between Cuba and Miami". *Latin American Perspectives*, *32*(1): 121-146.

Malinowski, B. *(1922) Argonauts of the Western Pacific.* London: Routledge.

Malkki, L.H. (2007). "Tradition and Improvisation in Ethnographic Field Research". *Improvising Theory. Process and Temporality in Ethnographic Field Work.* Eds. A. Cerwonka & L.H. Malkki. Chicago: University of Chicago Press, 162-188.

Marcus, G. E. (1995). "Ethnography in/of the World System: The Emergence of Multi-sited Ethnography." *Annual Review of Anthropology.* 24, 95-117.

McGee, R.J. & Warms, R.L. (2007). *Anthropological Theory - An Introductory History, Second Edition.* New York: McGraw-Hill Companies, Inc.

Menzies, W.W., & Menzies, R.P. (2000). *Spirit and power: Foundations of Pentecostal Experience.* Grand Rapids, MI: Zondervan.

Meyer, B. (1998). "Make a Complete Break with the Past: Memory and Post-Colonial Modernity in Ghanaian Pentecostalist Discourse". *Journal of Religion in Africa,* *28*(3), 316-349.

Miller, D. (2010). *Stuff.* Cambridge: Polity.

Molony, T.S.J. (2007). "Non-Developmental uses of mobile communication in Tanzania." *The Handbook of Mobile Communication Studies.* Ed. J.E. Katz. Cambridge MA: MIT.

Moore, H. L. (1999). *Anthropological Theory Today.* Cambridge: Polity Press.

Neitz M.J., Spickard J.V. (1990). "Steps Toward a Sociology of Religious Experience: The Theories of Mihaly Csikszentmihalyi and Alfred Schutz". *Sociological Analysis,* 51, 15-33.

Neocosmos, M. (2006) *From Foreign Natives to Native Foreigners: Explaining Xenophobia in Contemporary South Africa.* Dakar: CODESRIA.

Ng, K. H. (2002). Seeking the Christian tutelage: Agency and culture in Chinese immigrants' conversion to Christianity. *Sociology of Religion*, 63(2), 195-214.

Nkwi, W. G. (2009). "From the Elitist to the Commonality of Voice Communication: the History of the Telephone in Buea, Cameroon." *Mobile phones: The new talking drums of everyday Africa*. Eds. M. de Bruijn, F.B. Nyamnjoh & I. Brinkman. Langaa/ASC: Cameroon/ Leiden, 50-68.

Nyamnjoh, F.B. (2002). "A child is One Person's Only in the Womb": Domestication, Agency and Subjectivity in the Cameroonian Grassfields." *Postcolonial Subjectivities in Africa*. Eds. R. Werbner. London: Zed Books, 111-138.

Nyamnjoh, F.B. (2003). Chieftaincy and the Negotiation of Might and Right in Botswana Democracy. *Journal of Contemporary African Studies*, 21(2), 233-250.

Nyamnjoh, F.B. (2005). Images of Nyongo Amongst Bamenda Grassfielders in Whiteman Kontri. *Citizenship Studies*, 9(3), 241-269.

Nyamnjoh, F.B. (2006). *Insiders and Outsiders: Citizenship and Xenophobia in Contemporary Southern Africa*. Dakar: CODESRIA in association with Zed Books.

Nyamnjoh, F.B. (2007a). 'Ever-Diminishing Circles': The Paradoxes of Belonging in Botswana. Marisol de la Cadena & Orin Starn, (eds.), *Indigenous Experience Today*, 305-332.

Nyamnjoh, F.B. (2007b). From Bounded to Flexible Citizenship: Lessons from Africa. *Citizenship Studies*, *11*(1), 73-82.

Nyamnjoh, F.B. (2012a). Personal Communication: November 24, 2012.

Nyamnjoh, F.B. (2012b). Blinded by Sight: Divining the Future of Anthropology in Africa. *Africa Spectrum*, 47(2-3), 63-92.

Overing, J. & Passes, A. (2000). *The Anthropology of Love and Anger: The Aesthetics of Conviviality in Native Amazonia.* New York: Routledge.

Owen, J. (2011). *"On se Debrouille": Congolese Migrants' Search for Survival and Success in Muizenberg, Cape Town.* Thesis submitted for the fulfilment of the requirements for the degree of Doctor of Philosophy of Rhodes University: May 2011.

Paine, R. (1969). In Search of Friendship: An Exploratory Analysis in 'Middle-class' Culture. *Man*, 4(4), 505-524.

Palmer, C.T., Ellsworth, R.M., & Steadman, L.B. (2009). "Talk and Tradition: Why the Least Interesting Components of Religion may be the most Evolutionarily Important." *The Biological Evolution of Religious Mind and Behaviour.* Eds. E. Voland and W. Schiefenhvel. New York: Springer, 105-116.

Pastor Chris Online (2013). http://www.pastorchrisonline.org/home/intro/?ref=refe rred [accessed 25 July 2013].

Pelckmans, L. (2009). "Phoning Anthropologists: The Mobile Phone's (re-) Shaping of Anthropological Research". *Mobile Phones: The New Talking Drums of Everyday Africa.* Eds. M. de Bruijn, F.B. Nyamnjoh & I. Brinkman. Cameroon/ Leiden: Langaa/ASC, 23-49.

Piot, C. (2010). *Nostalgia for the Future: West Africa after the Cold War.* Chicago: University of Chicago Press.

Putnam, R. (2001). "Social capital: Measurement and consequences". *Canadian Journal of Policy Research*, 2(1), 41-51.

Sharp, J. (2008). ""Fortress SA": Xenophobic Violence in South Africa". *Anthropology Today*, Vol.24 (4): 1-3.

Sichone, O. (2003). "Together and Apart: African Refugees and Immigrants in Global Cape Town." *What Holds Us Together: Social Cohesion in South Africa.* Eds. D. Chidester, P. Dexter & W. James. Cape Town: HSRC, 120-140.

Sichone, O. (2008). Xenophobia and Xenophilia in South Africa: African Migrants in Cape Town. *Anthropology and the New Cosmopolitanism: Rooted, Feminist and Vernacular Perspectives,* Oxford: Berg Publishers.

Stark, R., & Finke, R. (2000). *Acts of Faith: Explaining the Human Side of Religion.* Berkeley/Los Angeles: University of California Press.

Van Binsbergen, W. (2004). "Can ICT belong in Africa, or is ICT Owned by the North Atlantic Region?". *Situating Globality: African Agency in the Appropriation of Global Culture.* Eds. *W.* van Binsbergen & R. van Dijk. Leiden: Brill, 107-146.

Verter, B. (2003). "Spiritual Capital: Theorizing Religion with Bourdieu against Bourdieu". *Sociological Theory,* 21(2), 150-174.

Wacquant, L.J. (Ed.) (2005). *Pierre Bourdieu and Democratic Politics: The Mystery of Ministry.* Cambridge/Malden, MA: Polity Press.

Warnier, J. P. (2006). Inside and outside: Surfaces and Containers. *Handbook of Material Culture.* Eds. C. Tilley, W. Keane, S. Küchler, M. Rowlands, & P. Spyer. London: SAGE Publications Ltd., 186-197

Warnier, J.P. (2009). "Technology as Efficacious Action on Objects... and Subjects". *Journal of Material Culture, 14*(4), 459-470.

Weston K. (1991). *Families We Choose: Lesbians, Gays, Kinship.* New York: Columbia University Press.

Williams, R. (2000) *Making Identity Matter: Identity, Society and Social Interaction.* Durham: Sociology Press.

Yang, F. (2004). "Gender and generation in a Chinese Christian Church". *Asian American Religions: The Making and Remaking of Borders and Boundaries.* Eds. T. Carnes and F. Yang (2004). New York University Press: New York, 205-22.

Zhao, S., Grasmuck, S., & Martin, J. (2008). Identity Construction on Facebook: Digital Empowerment in Anchored Relationships. *Computers in Human Behavior,* 24(5), 1816-1836.

www.ingramcontent.com/pod-product-compliance
Lightning Source LLC
Chambersburg PA
CBHW032354280326
41935CB00008B/566